BEHIND THE EXECUTIVE MASK

ALSO BY ALFRED J. MARROW:

Living Without Hate
Making Management Human

Foreign editions:
German—*Der Mensch Lebt Nicht Vom Lohn Allein*
Portuguese—*Administração Humanizada*
Dutch—*Naar Een Menselijke Bedrijfsleiding*
Hebrew— שנוי להנהלה אנושית
Japanese— 人間性の葛藤

Changing Patterns of Prejudice

BEHIND THE EXECUTIVE MASK

Greater Managerial Competence
Through Deeper Self-Understanding

ALFRED J. MARROW

AMERICAN MANAGEMENT ASSOCIATION

NEW YORK

This is No. 79 in the series
of AMA Management Reports.

DEDICATION

To the Harwood Manufacturing Corporation—whose officers and employees have influenced a whole generation of those interested in the application of scientific knowledge to management.

FOREWORD

"THERE IS NOTHING so practical," Kurt Lewin once said, "as a good theory." Now Alfred J. Marrow has, in this book, given further evidence of his life-long commitment to improve the world of practice with a clear vision of useful theory.

During my graduate student days at MIT, I became fascinated by Marrow, the psychologist-turned-businessman. He seemed to embody many of my own aspirations, particularly in his protean ability to fuse knowledge with action. Of course, many of us pay lip service to this commitment, but few have realized it so monumentally as Marrow, who, by dint of applying what he preaches as entrepreneur, has become a leading industrialist as well as a respected social scientist.

Marrow's commitment is based on two important assumptions. First, that there is no basic discontinuity between the scientist and the man of action. Both the scientist and the manager are required to "know what they are doing" if success is to be gained; both need similar skills of perception and diagnosis in order to understand the world around them.

7

The second assumption Marrow makes has to do with the role requirements of the manager. He can no longer be construed narrowly as a manager of a technological-financial system. He must be seen as being at the center of a highly complex and dynamic human network where he negotiates, transacts, and exchanges with a host of factors, external and internal, human and institutional. No longer is it possible to think of the manager as a specialist who pushes buttons according to some pre-programed instruction.

The new manager coordinates a social system, Marrow reasons; and if the enterprise is to succeed, the manager must develop keen eyes and ears for the human forces surrounding him upon whose resources the enterprise stands or falls. In short, the manager *must develop interpersonal competence,* an ability that is becoming less a luxury than a necessity in a time when human motivation is so crucial to success.

There is a third assumption that we can mention now, one that is intimately connected with the main focus of this book—namely, that these interpersonal and social skills cannot be learned solely through the traditional vehicles of classroom teaching or experience. The learning process Marrow describes is a complex mechanism whereby individuals come together and explore their experience, behavior, and assumptions about motivation in a laboratory setting. This means that they rely almost exclusively on their own dilemmas rather than on vicarious experiences; that they write their own book rather than "read the experts."

In other words, the participants—with the help of a trained leader—attempt to understand their own leadership behavior in a setting which is psychologically "safe" (that is, where risks can be taken without serious consequences). Learning in this laboratory setting has the advantages of (1) combining the intellectual and emotional components of administrative behavior; (2) providing an experience with men of similar positions, backgrounds, and human predicaments; and (3) fusing business practices with human motivation.

It is not easy to know what to call this form of learning. It is decidedly not "training" as we know it; nor is it "education" or "therapy" as these terms are typically used. The National Training Laboratories refers to it as "laboratory training," "group dynamics training," or "human relations training."

The name is unimportant. What is crucial and what Alfred J. Marrow constantly reminds us of is the growing significance of human dynamics in conducting the enterprise.

WARREN G. BENNIS
Professor of Industrial Management
Massachusetts Institute of Technology

INTRODUCTION

THERE SURELY ARE FEW MANAGERS in today's business world who would not agree that management is "getting things done through people." Certainly they have been told and told again that this is their basic job; that technical knowledge alone is not enough; that effective action presupposes effective motivation of subordinates and associates.

Just as the success of the company's product or service depends on consumer acceptance and goodwill, successful management depends on employee goodwill, which in turn is dependent on the relationships between human beings and must take into account their natural motives and desires. Trouble is inevitable where individual managers fail to realize that they may be less than perfect in this area or—worse—refuse to concede its importance.

It's not easy to admit to personal shortcomings of any kind, much less do something about them. It's far easier to assume a stubborn, belligerent, defensive attitude at the suggestion that there may be room for improvement. And many of us do adopt this attitude.

We all have the faults implicit in our virtues—and vice

versa. Thus the man who won't believe that the effect he has on others could be crippling his performance as a manager may also be depriving himself and his company of unsuspected and hence undeveloped strengths. And, with managerial talent increasingly at a premium, this is a loss which American industry can no longer afford.

There are few people as well equipped as Alfred J. Marrow to write this kind of book—a book that applies the findings and methods of the human sciences to the art of getting things done through people. To it he brings a rich combination of qualifications that is unique in this age of specialization. His standing as a distinguished psychologist is widely recognized. The esteem in which his work is regarded may be judged from his designation as 1964 winner of the Kurt Lewin Award, the highest honor in the field of social psychology.

Alfred J. Marrow is equally at home with the leaders of the American business community. He is the senior consultant to the American Management Association's Executive Action Course. He is a regular lecturer at the Management Course for Presidents given by the Presidents' Professional Association. He also serves as chairman of the board of the Harwood Manufacturing Corporation, the largest company within its specialized field in the textile industry.

Alfred J. Marrow's work thus serves as a bridge linking scientific knowledge of human behavior and the economic objectives of the company. His book offers a new kind of educational approach to the goals of improving managerial competence, increasing company profits, and enhancing human satisfactions.

The sensitivity training of which Dr. Marrow writes so persuasively is a tool of growing importance in helping managers to win the cooperation of the people they must work with and through. Here, in the give-and-take of actual situations, a man discovers the personal image he projects and sees how people react to it. More often than not this is a painful process, forcing him to break ingrained patterns of behavior and form new ones; yet a typical executive has called it "the most challenging and beneficial experience of my entire business career."

Companies everywhere have come to recognize the value of sensitivity training as an essential part of management development. I predict that the roster will continue to grow, that more companies will be rewarded in terms of improved "climate" and working relationships, and that more and more executives will know the satisfactions of increased personal effectiveness.

LAWRENCE A. APPLEY
President, American Management Association

CONTENTS

A WORD FROM THE AUTHOR •

UNTIL THE SECOND WORLD WAR the behavioral sciences showed little interest in the problems of business management. Insofar as they dealt with the subject at all, psychologists were concerned primarily with production workers. Little research was directed at the problems or the techniques of management.

In recent years, however, many systematic inquiries have been made of the factors which make for success in the management of people. Much research has been directed to the relationship between managerial approach, employee productivity, and job satisfaction. As a result, there is much less distrust between the managers of American business and the practitioners of modern psychology. Behavioral scientists and industrial leaders now know that they have much to learn from each other.

I have been personally privileged to participate in this collaboration between psychology and industry as a member of both groups. One of the early projects in this area —studies of leadership training for supervisors—began at the Harwood Manufacturing Company in 1942. Mine was a dual role as a member of management as well as a partner in the research done by my colleagues the late Kurt Lewin, and Alex Bavelas, and John R. P. French, Jr.

Several years later, in 1946, I collaborated with Kurt Lewin, Ronald Lippitt, and others in a leadership training workshop for the Connecticut Interracial Commission. The success of this venture soon led to the founding of the National Training Laboratories in Bethel, Maine.

My own concern with the application of sensitivity training or laboratory methods for re-educating executive behavior has continued through the years. In the companies with which I am associated I have seen at first hand how this laboratory method works and have observed the dramatic effect it has on attitudes and performance and in improved managerial competence. It has produced practical results in lower costs and higher productivity.

As senior consultant to the Executive Action Course of the American Management Association, I have had the opportunity to see lab training develop into a major tool of management. Over the years I have closely observed the work of the National Training Laboratories and have understood the reasons for its pre-eminent position in this field. I agree with Edgar H. Schein that it "is constantly advancing the frontiers of knowledge and has included some of the most exciting contributions to the field of human relations training."

I have seen the highly significant innovations of Robert R. Blake and Jane S. Mouton in their instrumented training lab at the University of Texas and of Robert Tannenbaum, Fred Massarik, and the late Irving Weschler at the University of California, where they have developed new ways of helping "the individual in his desires—to know himself more intimately—to find a more significant meaning for his life."

Today there are many kinds of labs, many different approaches, different purposes, different expectations. New methods are constantly being tried. Existing knowledge and data are not adequate, I feel, to argue for any one viewpoint or any particular method of lab training. But this book will describe what happens in a typical lab for training managerial personnel of business establishments, one that is known to have produced excellent results. At times the things that happen are not what we expect. But this, too, is part of the laboratory experience—part of learning how to learn.

One thing we have discovered is that sensitivity training cannot help everybody. Its value will vary from individual to individual and company to company. The matter usually boils down to the attitude of people toward changing beliefs and practices. But we have learned that most people can benefit, that in the training lab the majority of people can learn and grow and help their companies to solve problems. We have seen them come from small companies and large ones. They have been board chairmen of giant corporations and plant managers of small companies. What they share in common—a desire to improve their skills in working through people—transcends the size of their companies or the titles they hold.

I have tried to avoid the jargon of the social scientist as much as possible. Ultimately, I think, the scientific vocabulary will become a part of our daily communications. For the present, however, the language of the manager and the lexicon of the behavioral scientist are still too far apart. I hope this book will provide one more link between the two and bring a little closer the science of behavior and the management of men.

The printed page can never capture the orchestration of feeling that comes to each participant in a sensitivity training group. So much happens at the same time, so many different attitudes and actions need to be observed, that no description can do justice to the experience. To know what life in a training laboratory is like, it is necessary to attend one. This, I hope, many of my readers will feel impelled to do.

I have drawn upon the ideas of so many individuals and used so many sources that it would be impossible for me to acknowledge them all by specific references. I am grateful to those people—in industry and in social science—whose collaboration made possible the development of the theory and practice of laboratory training for industry.

There are, however, a few persons who must be mentioned. Among these was my close friend and teacher, Kurt Lewin, one of the greatest figures in psychology in this century, whose brilliant concepts led to the development of action research and the field of group dynamics.

I am deeply indebted to my dear friend Horace M. Kallen, with whom I have shared a common commitment that has bound us together for many years. His vigorous criticism led to many valuable revisions of the manuscript.

I wish to thank Gilbert David and Robert Pearse, whose long experience in laboratory training for executives proved of great value in the preparation of the various drafts of the manuscript.

I profited from the suggestions of a number of colleagues who read a preliminary draft of portions of the manuscript. They are Warren G. Bennis, Edwin M. Glasscock, Kenneth H. Recknagel, Charles Roth, and Nathaniel N. Noble.

I am grateful to Richard Cohen for stimulating criticism and perceptive and wise editorial guidance and wish to thank Beatrice Pelzer who conscientiously supervised the secretarial preparation of the manuscript.

CHAPTER I

THE EXECUTIVE'S DILEMMA •

THE WORLD WE LIVE and work in is in a process of sudden change; it is a world of technological revolution and of scientific breakthroughs. These confront management with unprecedented problems. Once dependable ways of conducting business no longer seem to work, nor do traditional methods of dealing with people.

Customary ways of handling problems—mounting costs, for one—frequently fail to achieve the desired result: raising prices to increase profits may simply result in losing customers. Acquiring or merging with other businesses may either turn out too costly or be too slow in bringing results. Automation and data processing—the new panaceas of the 1960's—have their own built-in drawbacks.

But the greatest challenge which confronts the profit-conscious executive in the handling of people, particularly his managerial staff. How can he turn the managers on his staff into a real "team"—a group of men who work well and enthusiastically with one another, who pull for the company, and not merely each for himself? How can they be led to understand their joint as well as their individual functions in the enterprise so that responsibility is best met and authority most effectively exercised? And how, finally, can this be done in terms of managerial control and the carrying out of company plans and policies? These questions reveal that the task of management has become more complex. In fact it is more difficult than at any time since the Industrial Revolution.

In the apparently simple matter of maintaining leadership, the Brookings Institution reports that of the 100 leading American companies in 1909, only 36 remained among the top group in 1948. Despite their established reputations, financial resources, and technical know-how, 64 of the top 100 companies failed to retain their high place in the course of a single generation. Those companies which did not had in some way failed to meet the needs of people—the people they dealt with, whether they were workers, customers, or managers.

Again, in the matter of external growth through acquisition, a recent study indicates that as many as two-thirds of all acquisitions completed during a five-year period are still unprofitable. Why? Mainly because of unanticipated difficulties in integrating the *personnel* of the acquired business into the parent organization.

Or take the matter of internal growth. It has been found that big companies must grow bigger and small companies must become big, or they will both go out of business. Yet the faster a company grows, the more new people it must employ and train at every operational level. The more new people, the more problems of coordination, communication, and organization. The larger a company, the more difficult it becomes to keep up the traditional forms of authority, leadership, and control. Large organizations, especially, sooner or later reach the point where they begin to question whether the goals and needs of the individual can be so integrated with the goals and needs of the firm that what is best for the individual is also best for the company.

THE HEART OF THE PROBLEM

In the past, managerial control rested on the authority-obedience relationship between the manager and his subordinates. But in these days we see that tight control has the effect of limiting rather than stimulating productivity; and greater efficiency, profits, and growth seem to call for a different kind of approach. Today's manager, whether the head of a huge corporation or the supervisor of eight delivery men, is learning the limited power of control by coercion, for such control eventually causes conflict, apathy, and resistance.

However completely mechanized and automated our economy may be, it remains more than ever management's task to learn how to get the best out of people. This means that management must understand the motives of people, must study what effect organizational policies have on the mature individual, and must know how best to communicate with him. The productivity and profits of a business follow from the teamwork of its personnel, from the management of men—not from handling machines.

The present level of human productivity in American companies—which authorities estimate as only 50 per cent of potential—is today an anachronism. It is shocking to realize that the vaunted "efficiency" of our industrial economy results in our getting only 50 per cent of the possible performance out of our work force. If an improvement of only 10 per cent could be attained, the reduction in cost would be phenomenal. And such an increase is possible without vast capital expenditures for automated equipment, which has at best an uncertain payoff period. The task is one of reshaping the company's policies and its managerial approaches to fit the body of knowledge produced by the behavioral sciences in researches which show how people can be motivated to perform at their best. This knowledge discloses more reliably than ever why men act as they do:

- We know much more about what they crave and what they fear; what they are moved by and what they remain indifferent to.
- We understand why some men work hard and others do not; why some supervisors get high production and others do poorly.
- We know why some forms of communication fail and others succeed; how management practices can directly affect absenteeism due to sickness and accident.
- We can see more clearly than ever what helps and what hinders innovation and creativity.

This body of knowledge is available to the modern business executive for solution of the problems that keep him and his company from realizing their full potential. Use of it means more than a mere shift in focus from physical production to human relations, more than merely spending less time on the machines and more time on the men. It means, in addition, looking into the authoritarian attitudes of most organizations, for these attitudes breed conflict. It means changing present practices so that conflict will give way to cooperation.

One method is to stop trying to "sell" the company to

its employees and try instead to get its managers to re-examine their ideas and attitudes about what makes for effective management. The average manager's answer to the question of who is to be changed is that it is the workers or his boss. He doesn't think of changing himself.

The behavioral sciences now challenge this attitude. Research suggests changing the approach at all three levels of management—first-line supervisors, middle management, and top executives. This, research tells us, should come first. If these men are to give genuine leadership, they need to know a lot more about their motives, their values, their emotional maturity, and the impact they make on the men they work with. With this self-knowledge, with the better attitudes it brings, will come improved attitudes in subordinates. Self-knowledge is a business necessity if the manager is to develop the cooperative relationships which will turn his subordinates into a working team with good morale and high motivation.

A first step, therefore, is for the man who manages others to take a good close look at himself; to follow the ancient precept to "know thyself." He must examine his attitudes, recognize his inadequacies and failings, and then reshape them into new insights and skills. This discovery and reshaping of the self is at the heart of that re-education which management needs today. As Chris Argyris put it, "It is impossible to understand others unless we understand ourselves, and we cannot understand ourselves unless we understand others."

THE SOLUTION PROPOSED

There is a valuable instrument for acquiring this knowledge. It is a dramatic development known by a number of names, none of which fully describes its character:

sensitivity training, laboratory training, or laboratory education.

Designed by leaders in the behavioral sciences, it has many variations and many institutional arrangements. The first training center was established in 1947 at Bethel, Maine, by the National Training Laboratories under the joint sponsorship of the Research Center for Group Dynamics at the Massachusetts Institute of Technology and the National Education Association. Cooperating were Cornell University and the University of California. Bethel continues to be the principal laboratory training center in the United States and now has about 4,500 alumni. In the years since its founding, National Training Laboratories, whose objective is "building bridges between the social scientist and the practitioner attempting to apply scientific knowledge in day-to-day problems," has become the world center for research and training in human relations under the leadership of Leland P. Bradford.

A number of others followed suit: the American Management Association with its Executive Action Course, of whose 2,000 alumni about 150 have been company presidents; Standard Oil Company of New Jersey with a somewhat larger number; Robert R. Blake and Jane S. Mouton of the University of Texas, who have trained about 3,000 executives in their Managerial Grid Program; and UCLA, where Robert Tannenbaum, Fred Massarik, and the late Irving Weschler provided the necessary guidance. Training labs are being sponsored or are in use in more than 40 educational centers in the United States, including Boston University, Columbia, Harvard, Massachusetts Institute of Technology, Michigan, the University of Chicago, Yale, and many more.

This type of training differs from that usually provided in the classroom, the seminar, or the workshop. For one thing, the subject matter is not a body of knowledge but a body of men, and this subject matter is not so much learned as experienced. For another, the emphasis is on changing individual conduct rather than on imparting scientific knowledge.

Sensitivity training is often called laboratory training because it encourages the individual to examine his own behavior and to experiment with new ways of relating to others. The subjects of the experiment are also the participants. The training laboratory is the special environment in which they learn new things about themselves. The participant is in the unique position of being at the same time both the experimenter and the subject of the experiment.

The experience is frequently a deeply moving one. It often means a re-evaluation of a lifetime of values and beliefs. It is a kind of emotional re-education. It teaches that the modern executive to be truly efficient must understand as much about feelings as he does about facts: that logic is never enough. Many executives think that they subscribe to this proposition. In the training lab, they may discover that in actual practice they do not.

Here the trainees analyze each other's attitudes, react to each other's behavior, compare the way they perceive themselves with the way they appear to the world. A man may learn that far from being objective, he is biased in his judgment of himself and in his relation to others. But he may also learn that he possesses inner resources and powers which he hasn't been using. Sensitivity training awakens them, starts them functioning.

It is this new understanding of himself combined with new skills in dealing with others and new insights into company organization that helps the trainee to solve problems such as the following:

Our staff meetings seldom accomplish anything. We meet once a week to iron out really pressing problems, but the discussion invariably runs in circles. The trouble with these men is that they all have their own specialized interests and won't listen to one another. We're wasting valuable time this way, and a lot of friction is developing, too.

How can I keep a valuable young executive in line and not offend him? Our company made special concessions to get this man. We were convinced he had a lot to offer us, and we still are. The fact that he's behaving like a maverick is hurting him and it's hurting us. We want to keep him. I hate the thought of losing him to a competitor. But we can't keep him unless he changes his attitude. What can I do to help this man understand that he's working for a company, not for his own ego?

I can't get two division managers to work together. My sales and production heads refuse to see each other's point of view. Right now my company is 30 days late on production of our most popular models, just because these men didn't synchronize their schedules. It seems to be a problem that could have been avoided in the beginning by a little cooperation.

How can I reason with an old-timer? This man has been with the company for 30 years, and his experience is really valuable. But it's impossible to get him to budge an inch from his own way of doing things. I've been trying to get him to introduce a new work simplification plan in his department for months. If only he would try it for one week, he'd be sold on it completely.

Why won't my assistant level with me? I've heard from other sources that he's dissatisfied. More than once I've talked to him, told him I wanted to help, asked him to confide in me. Every time he's clammed up. Why should he tell others when he won't tell me?

Sensitivity training is designed to help good managers become better managers. Participants are successful people seeking more effective ways of using and improving their management skills. Executives who have participated in a laboratory training program have testified to the benefit they derived in learning to explore their own motives, feelings, relationships, and behavior and to experiment with new ways of behaving.

CHAPTER II

WHAT IS LABORATORY TRAINING? •

DURING THE PAST FIVE YEARS nearly ten thousand managers have shared the challenging and rewarding experience of the training laboratory. Yet on their return to their homes and offices, they have found it a difficult thing to describe.

If we ask the executive who has recently attended such a course, "What is it like?" he is likely to reply, "Difficult at first. But very interesting. Very." If we press him further, "Yes, but what did you do? How does it work?" the man usually ponders a moment, tries to formulate a description that will convey the essence of the experience in terms his questioner will really understand—and then finds there is no easy way to do it. Nor can we find a satisfactory description in print outside the technical literature, for in spite of the tremendous influence which this unique form of training has already had on the lives of thousands of executives, little has been written about it for the business community.

A laboratory training course may run anywhere from four days to four weeks, although a program of several weeks is most common. For the sake of convenience, we have chosen to describe here a program designed to cover three weeks. The important thing, however, is the goal sought; this determines the amount of time devoted to achieving it.

During the first week the emphasis is on the individual. The goal is to foster in the participant (1) a greater insight into self and an awareness of the impact of self on other people and (2) an increased sensitivity to the feelings of others and a better understanding of the behavior of others and how this affects the participant.

In the second week, the emphasis shifts to the group: the forces that operate in a group, the effectiveness of the participant as a group member and leader, and the roles that need to be played in building and maintaining the group. In other words, the trainee learns how groups take shape, grow, and function.

Finally, in the third week attention is focused on organizational effectiveness, motivation, leadership, and managing change. The participant is helped to gain a greater understanding of how company organization affects individual effectiveness and group functioning and how a collaborative atmosphere within an organization can be established. The goal is for the trainee to leave the course with a plan for back-home application of what he has learned in the first two weeks to his own management problems or to those in the company generally.

In any one week, the meetings held are of three general types: the T-group, the skill session, and the general session. The T-group is the basic unit and consists of eight to fifteen participants—ten being the usual number. The skill session is the T-group meeting to perform specific exercises like role playing: it is task-oriented. The general session includes the entire group of trainees assembled for lectures or demonstrations.

Most of the meetings are confined to the T-group. For instance, in one type of sensitivity training the T-group meets every day during the first week; there is one skill session; and an average of three general sessions are held.

The training center is very often in an isolated setting; but even if it is in the heart of a large city, it is a kind of cultural island physically removed from the distractions of job and family.

In most courses of this type, no two members of the same company or of directly competitive companies are assigned to the same T-group. At some training centers, however, groups of managers from a single company come together for training in what are called family groups. These may be further divided into groups of men on the same management level or groups consisting of several levels.

The trainee may have made his own decision to attend, or he may have been sent by the firm that employs him. He may know something about laboratory training from talking with colleagues who have undergone training before, or he may come to the lab "cold" and be quite unprepared for the experience he's about to have.

"I'm here," one new member says, "at the request of the company, and frankly I don't know what I expect to get out of it. I've talked to people who weren't able to tell me what it's all about after they've been here a whole week. So if *they* can't tell me, or can't explain it, how can I be expected to figure it out in advance?"

To this he adds, "Several men in our company who have attended seem to have acquired a kind of deep understanding among themselves. They don't talk much about it, but they do act differently—more cooperative, I would say."

When someone suggests that it sounds as though "they were initiated into something," he replies, "That's how they seem, perhaps unintentionally. It's as though they've learned something useful that I don't know."

In any case, the first thing the trainee does is attend an orientation session which brings together the entire group of 50 or 60 trainees. Here the men are given their schedule: T-group sessions morning, afternoon, and evening, interspersed with skill sessions and occasional general theory sessions that are attended by the entire group. Before they leave the assembly hall, they are divided into T-groups.

Each T-group has its own professional leader, usually a trained social psychologist. But the leader does not exert control; he serves, rather, as a catalyst and guide to channel the group into the most productive learning situations. The T-group is an unstructured, self-directed group with no predetermined agenda to cover. There are no fixed rules: the group makes its own rules in a highly permissive atmosphere.

Experience has shown that the lack of structure heightens the sensitivity of the participants to one another's behavior and enables them to become aware of their own insensitivities and distortions. It also sharpens their interest in their fellow trainees: what kind of people they are, which ones they feel they will come to like, which ones they will come to dislike. As the sessions continue and feedback develops, changes of attitude follow. Whatever variations have been introduced in the rapid growth and extension of sensitivity training—and there are many—the use of the unstructured group remains a standard feature of the training lab.

Most of what the trainees learn in the T-group meetings they learn from one another rather than the lab staff. The interaction of the participants with each other is a distinctive element of the daily sessions. The emphasis in the training lab is not on lectures, though there are some. It is not on reading material, though this is part of the course. Rather the emphasis is on the group itself: its history (what happens to it from the time the members first come together), its composition (the men who make it up, how they act individually, and how they behave together). From the very first session, the participants are put on their own; the agenda—if it can be called that— is provided by the dilemmas that develop in the process of building a group. This happens to them without their being told what to do, who is in charge, what to talk about, or who should say it.

Another important feature is feedback. Trainees are constantly urged to look back and see what their behavior has revealed. For instance, in the beginning some may have been overly anxious or impatient to get started. Some may have played it safe, said nothing, and thus contributed nothing. Some may have shown a need to dominate the meeting and organize the group. "We can't just *sit* here," a member may say. "Now, *I*'ll tell you what we'll do. . . ." And what he has said is on the record, to be studied. In subsequent sessions the men analyze their own experiences in the struggle to create a working group: the way one member tried to control the group, the three-man clique that railroaded a decision on how to fill the time, the chairman they elected who couldn't cope with some of the members.

A third characteristic of the T-group is the candor and

the sense of intimacy generated. The executives who make up the T-group find themselves alone together, like people on a raft. One moment they are strangers who have just met. The thing they do know about each other is that they are all there to help not only themselves but everyone else. However, this is enough to create quickly an atmosphere of mutual confidence and trust. Eventually, they tell each other how they feel and what they see—frankly, freely, and fully. They learn to communicate their feelings more accurately.

This does not mean there won't be disagreement and criticism. In fact, it almost guarantees that there will be. Sometimes the disagreement will be emphatic and sharp. However, that is how it should be for the good of the learning process. For one of the aims of the training laboratory is to learn how to deal with conflict constructively—neither to suppress it nor to try to eliminate it. One measure of a man's progress is how he accepts this criticism—how well he takes it—without hostility, defensiveness, or a tendency to retaliate.

Gradually, members of the T-group unlearn the inappropriate reactions and find the courage to experiment with new responses. They gain confidence as they learn to see themselves in less distorted ways. Learning anything new and different is seldom easy. But the unlearning and relearning of attitudes and beliefs that occur in a T-group may be frustrating and in a sense even painful—although both may in the end turn out to be highly exhilirating and deeply satisfying.

CHAPTER III

THE IMPORTANT FIRST MEETING •

THE SETTING LOOKS PEACEFUL enough: a pine-paneled room in an isolated country resort, with a fine view from the picture window. But as the ten men begin filing into the room, taking their places at the large round table, the atmosphere seems charged. One senses a kind of uneasiness, the sort of anxiety that goes with expecting something unprecedented. The men contribute to it in varying ways: to what degree depends on what each man really *is* and not on what he *appears to be*.

The men are informally dressed in sport shirts and slacks. Each places his name card on the table in front of him and takes his chair. Some have an easy air, but appearances are often deceptive. Some look around as though they are about to give an order for lunch and are already convinced the service will be slow.

34

When all members are assembled, the leader may say:

Now, I'd like to say a few words. You'll find that I'm a leader who isn't doing much leading. This will be especially true during the early part of the week.

Our aim—our deliberate purpose—is to place you in an open-ended, unstructured situation so that you can organize yourselves as a group as freely as possible and decide for yourselves what is important for you to work on. Design your program in whatever way you feel will be most advantageous to you.

My own role for the present is mostly that of catalyst, helping when and where I can but in no sense directing or building your program.

Perhaps you'll find today or maybe tomorrow that you feel frustrated because there isn't enough structure to the proceedings. Maybe later in the week you'll ask me, "If it's supposed to happen this way, why didn't you tell us?" Well I *am* telling you, now. And I am also telling you that later in the week you'll say I really didn't.

Let me repeat: It's your program. I'll step in from time to time. I'll make my comments on what you're doing, on what's happening.

Occasionally I may ask you to stop to take ratings—to give your reactions to the sessions as a whole and to each other.

One more thing: In sensitivity training we concentrate on what we call the "here and now"—how you act and react in the lab. We're interested in your childhood or your attitudes toward your family or any of your past experiences only as they directly relate to your self-understanding in the interactions that occur here.

Remember, I won't be telling you what to do or be trying to influence what you do.

I think I should say one final thing. This week will be useful and valuable to the extent that you become involved in the proceedings. You can, of course, remain passive. But it isn't likely that you'll get as much out of them. Only participation can bring the results you hope for in joining this lab. Learning is like eating: no one can do it for you; you must do it for yourself.

That's all for right now. I'll end with an old cliché: You'll get as much out of this training as you put into it.

A popular way of getting a T-group going after the introductory remarks of the leader is for the group to accept some individual suggestions that they introduce themselves to each other. This is generally approved with some enthusiasm by several—especially those who are uneasy about the initial lack of form.

The introductions begin (who started them and why will be analyzed later), and the men generally take turns around the table. At times, members may ask each other further questions. Usually the self-introductions are a recital of impersonal facts: size of company, products, number of employees, volume, previous employment history, and the like.

THE UNSTRUCTURED GROUP

It is at this point that one of the men breaks the ice by asking questions. Let's call him Ken. He started drumming on the table as soon as he sat down.

"Well," he says, "what now? What do we do? Who is chairman? What are the assignments?"

Nobody answers him. He stares at the leader. "How about it, Steve?"

The leader shrugs, still smiling. "It's up to the group."

Ken doesn't realize that it really *is* up to the group. He

is a man with a powerful drive. It brought him where he is—chief executive of an electric-components firm. He demands to get going as always. But just now he's trying to curb his impatience. He senses that's the thing to do, however difficult.

He can't help going on. "Then who takes over?" he asks, looking around. He sees that others, executives like himself and accustomed to getting down to business quickly, are also impatient. He expresses their feelings, too, though perhaps they wouldn't want to admit it. Some of the men seem secretly amused; yet this may be only because they sense in Ken's actions a projection of their own impatience, their own frustrations.

Steve, the group leader, merely replies, "No one person is in charge here, really. It's up to you."

Ken tries again. "Well, what the heck, isn't there an agenda or plan? Isn't there some kind of general procedure?"

Steve answers, "The group can do whatever it wants."

Now Ken sounds and looks very irritated.

Then George speaks up. He is the president of a firm that makes kitchen equipment. This is the first time he and Ken have met. But when George speaks, he sounds as though he has known Ken—or people like him—all his life.

"I think he means, Ken, that we make our own rules— that is, if we're going to have any. Is that right, Steve?"

Steve nods. "For the present, let's say that's about it."

Ken stares around at the others. He can't quite believe it. Then he laughs, drily. "Well, for Pete's sake, is that what my firm is paying out good money for?"

A chuckle comes from around the table. Ken's comment relieves some of the tension. But the laughter, though good-natured, is in part at Ken's expense, and he is smart enough to know it. He is wondering why he is so much more disturbed by the lack of set procedures than most of the others seem to be. He wants to find out but realizes it won't be easy. But maybe that just shows it's something he really ought to know more about.

The unstructured, permissive character of the T-group is important because it creates dilemmas that will uncover a person's strengths and weaknesses. These are often noted by people who know him but rarely discussed with him in ordinary social relationships. The patternlessness of the T-group throws its members back on their established habits of dealing with stress and thus serves to reveal the man whom the mask of manners conceals. One might compare the lack of structure in the T-group to a Rorschach inkblot in which a person sees what he puts there.

The start of a T-group program has also been compared to a vacuum. The vacuum is filled by the reactions of the group members to the dilemma of the unstructured situation: their annoyance, confusion, resentment, puzzlement. This behavior provides the raw material for comment, analysis, and criticism by the trainees themselves.

The focus is on the group process itself and the behavior of its members in reacting to the dilemma. By examining and studying their own reactions and hearing comments and interpretations from others, the men acquire new insights into themselves and the way they affect other people. They also learn they are not alone in their fears and feelings of inadequacy.

What rises to the surface is not so much the intellectual ability of the lab participant as his emotional make-up. It is feeling, not just fact, that the T-group deals with. How does Ken react to the absence of an agenda? How is George affected by Ken's reaction? What is the source of Joe's response: dominance or deference or defensiveness?

Each member of the group will react to the dilemma in his own way; will compete for control of the group or let someone else take over; will cooperate with his fellows or play the lone wolf; will wait patiently for something to happen or explode first.

It is for these reasons that the T-group's first morning is perhaps the one which causes the most anxiety. Some react by talking too much; some talk too little. To the group leader's insistence that he is there mainly to help interpret their own actions, the dependent members are prone to show resentment or hostility.

One says, "This doesn't make any sense to me."

Another complains, "I might as well go back to my office. We don't seem to be getting anywhere. I have too much work piled up to be wasting my time here."

A third man asks, "Are we supposed to sit around and twitch?"

Still another says, "I wish I could get my money back. But since I can't, let's run the session ourselves. The leader is no help. If he gets paid for doing nothing, I'd like to become a psychologist myself."

From the leader, resentment may turn toward other trainees when one declares, "We need a chairman to get this thing off the ground," and assumes the chairmanship himself.

Another may ask, "Who put *you* in charge?" This may bring a laugh, but it nevertheless conveys the challenge to arbitrary, unauthorized action.

Not every lab participant feels anxious about the lack of agenda. One T-group member may agree at once that it is best not to have a ready-made structure.

"I'm in no hurry to get organized," he says. "There's too much organization in my daily life. Too much structure. Me, I don't mind this free way of moving. I like it."

But the man next to him says, "Look, we're paid to run an organization; yet we can't even organize a bunch of talented executives. What's wrong with us? Something must be."

A typical comment at this point is, "Why doesn't someone tell us what to do?"

The truth is that each man must find out for himself or defeat the purpose of joining the T-group. He may discover, for example, that the present cause of his emotional stress comes from the efforts of some individual—or a small clique—to control the meeting and that this keeps him from exercising the kind of control to which he is accustomed. This is important to him. But what is he to do about it? Will he fight back? Will he give in? Or is there a third way which might prove satisfactory to everybody?

THE IMPORTANCE OF FEEDBACK

Since all observations are made to the entire group, there is a minimum of partiality or distortion when the time comes to discuss what was said and how it was heard. What was the effect of Joe's reaction to criticism, Frank's discomfort with emotion, or Jerry's need to make compromises? Broad agreement or near unanimity among the members about negative feelings toward one individual's behavior carries a powerful impact.

The give and take, the exchange of feelings, is called "feedback." Through feedback, the lab trainees express their reactions to one another's behavior frankly and freely. It is the kind of reaction they would rarely express in daily interpersonal relations.

"Ken, you intimidate me," says Charles. "You get sarcastic. You sulk when anyone disagrees with you. When you walk into the room, I feel like standing at attention and saluting. I wonder if your employees feel that way."

Ken answers, "I certainly don't want them to."

"Don't you?" Charles continues. "I wonder if you really know how you want them to feel. And I wonder if you know as much about what's going on in your company as you think you do."

Then, again, it may be Ken who is the critic and Charles who is on the receiving end.

"Charles, why do you go on pretending that you're so damned relaxed? You're nowhere near as calm and collected as you pretend to be."

"What makes you say that?"

"Why, it's obvious. You talk about keeping cool, but you have a lot of nervous habits. You talk about being happy with your family and happy in your job; yet some of the things you let slip this morning and the way you said them make me feel you have a grudge against the world."

Charles shakes his head. "You couldn't be more wrong."

"Come on, Charles. Why not be honest with yourself? If you're mad or impatient or angry, let it come out. Why pretend to be what you aren't?"

Charles answers sharply, "You don't have to worry about ulcers. You're not the type that gets them. You just give them."

There is a laugh, and someone else gives his reaction to the way both Charles and Ken shared their feelings about each other.

As they develop the candor and spontaneity typical of the T-group, expression becomes freer. As they learn together, it becomes easier for them to accept honest criticism without becoming angry and without wanting to hit back.

"Harry," one member remarks, "every time somebody objects to a suggestion you've made, you try to wisecrack your way out of it."

And Harry retorts, "How do *you* think I ought to respond when somebody knocks down my suggestions?"

"I'll tell you what *I* would do," Joe answers. "I'd try to answer the objection."

"Maybe you would," says Harry, "but your tone and manner when you knock down a suggestion aren't very constructive. You haven't said anything constructive yet. Or friendly, either."

Then, suddenly, another member is at the receiving end of the comment. Joe says, "Maybe you think I ought to pull into my shell the way Dave here has. He hasn't opened his mouth yet."

Dave looks startled. It's true that he hasn't contributed very much, but he didn't think anyone noticed it.

"How about it, Dave?" Joe continues, "I'd like to hear how you feel about my tone and manner. You're not contributing a thing by just sitting there."

There's a chuckle, and now it's up to Dave. He must either speak up or acknowledge as true the implication that he hasn't much to contribute.

So he speaks up, and the others begin to find out what he is really like as a person.

Feedback can perform its functions quickly. It may begin with a few halting and polite comments on somebody's behavior. But soon it shapes up as free, candid, and good-natured give and take; it provides members of the group with more information about themselves than they would normally receive in a lifetime. And feedback brings to each participant a different, more realistic image of himself than he brought to the group.

The fact that in the beginning the members of the

T-group are strangers to one another reduces the likelihood of any one man's defending himself by accusing others of self-serving motives. The initial response, however, is often a more or less inverse candor. Members find it easier to expose others than to expose themselves. At first, candor is disturbing; it arouses puzzlement or resentment which then must be accounted for to the entire group.

THE DEVELOPMENT OF CANDOR

After observing a training lab, the noted theoretical psychologist A. H. Maslow reported as follows:

> My very first impression was one of real shock and amazement. These people behaved and talked in a spontaneous and free way that I have associated . . . with people who have been under psychoanalysis for a year or two at least. . . . I've always assumed that any change in character is going to take two or three years to make. Well, apparently it can happen a lot faster, very much faster in this kind of social situation. I guess this is the most important change that I carry away with me from the experience.

The following is the kind of exchange that illustrates what Professor Maslow may have had in mind.

DAVE: I admit it. I'm not good at leading, not comfortable asserting myself over others. I feel better and think I work better under someone else.

FRED: What's your idea of a good leader?

DAVE: Frankly, not someone like you. You hold yourself too detached and aloof. No warmth comes through. You make decisions without consulting the rest of us. You don't make us feel as if we're on the team. You prefer being in control. I need to identify with the man I work for, to feel I'd want to be like him, to share his ideas. I couldn't feel that way with you. I think I'd always feel a barrier. I'm glad I told you that. I was really speaking for myself. I don't think I've ever spoken this freely before to anyone without being angry.

Since Freud, it has been commonly recognized that the basic drives in behavior lie deep in man's unconscious. Sensitivity training, however, has given proof that the way a person behaves toward others and his awareness of himself can be influenced by the social environment in which he works and lives. It also shows that the psychoanalytic form of probing is not necessary in order to expose this behavior.

Any learning process is made easier when outside distractions are removed. This is the value of the isolated setting of laboratory training. Living, eating, relaxing together, the trainees get to know one another well—often intimately—in a brief time. One day they are strangers looking somewhat apprehensively at each other around a conference table. The next they are treating each other as close friends of long standing.

Ken is speaking again, getting something off his chest about the executives he's got working for him. "No one wants to take responsibility. I don't get it. When I was coming up through the ranks, I took on every added responsibility I could. Now I'm in a position to delegate authority, and what happens? My subordinates think I'm kidding. I do two or three times as much work as I should."

Another member asks simply, "Why?"

"I just told you why. Besides, I can't think of one man I could really trust to take over."

"Ken, I think you've answered your own question. You don't trust them, so they don't trust you. I think you've made them afraid of you."

At this point, Ted changes the subject.

"Why," he asks, "do the same problems keep coming up? Just when we think we've got a problem licked, it pops up again in another area."

"Well," says George, "Maybe it isn't enough to know how to deal with the problem *after* it comes up."

"What do you mean by that?"

"The idea is to spot trouble before it happens. To do that, you need to develop the kind of management team that will be able to come to you with ideas and suggestions that will prevent the problems from coming up at all."

Ted agrees. "That's something to think about. But how do you get them to come to you? The trouble with my people is that they keep hiding bad news from me—or try to—until it's too late."

THE TRAINING LEADER

So far we have not put much stress on the role of the training leader. He is, of course, a key figure, and his work requires more skill than at first seems obvious. The initial role of this apparently neutral observer (a psychologist with special training) is not as easy as it appears. For while he seems to be doing almost nothing during the first hours of the T-group—when the men "need" him most—he is in fact watching, getting to know them, and subtly gauging the development of the group from a collection of individuals to something with a personality of its own.

Only when the leader feels the men are beginning to outgrow their dependence on him—when he sees them designing a procedure, devising an agenda—does he become more active. He may suggest, for example, that they speak out with greater candor and less caution—although he never says anything he believes the group should say for itself.

For instance, a member asks him how other groups get started. He answers, "By themselves. The same as you."

"Are they all as confused as we are?"

He answers with a question. "Are you confused? Why? Perhaps everybody would like to know."

His apparent noncooperation may bring sharp criticism from the group. He not only doesn't object to the frankness but encourages it. He is not an instructor who tells students what to do and how to do it. He exercises no authority and calls for no deference. His teaching is by example, particularly in the way he accepts criticism without resentment, defense, or excuse.

The leader's ability to handle anger and anxiety directed at him is especially important during the early days of the group, when frustrations and tensions are high. In receiving these emotional reactions calmly, he helps make the men aware that they too can speak frankly to one another about their responses and hear what is said calmly. His example says, in effect, "You see? You criticize me. But I don't resent it. I'm interested to know what you think of me, no matter what you think."

Each T-group, as it develops and grows, makes its own history. The leader must be alert to the moments in this history when the trainees show that they are beginning to acquire a better understanding of themselves and of their relationships to others. When he sees this understanding being attained, the leader switches to helping the men apply their new insights to the actual problems they will encounter back at their work, for it is behavior that the lab seeks to change. New understandings or new insights alone are not enough. They must be followed by improvements back on the job in managerial competence.

Ken having spoken, the leader may ask, "Why do you think Ken said that?"

Another man answers, "I think he still feels touchy and doesn't realize it."

"Then you think it's—what?"

"I think it's a defense, as it was a while ago with George here."

Then the leader may turn to Ken. "How about it? Do you still feel resentful?"

The leader earns the support of the group because he shows that as leader he neither rejects nor punishes, neither penalizes nor tries to embarrass anyone. The trainees are on his side because they know he is on theirs. He helps them learn how to understand what they are really like and what their real impact on others is.

The leader's competence is of crucial importance to the success of the individual and group learning in the lab training experience. With the lightest touch he can stir hostility or create a new dilemma. His mere presence poses an issue for the group to deal with. To those members with strong dependency needs, he is someone to lean on; to those with hostility to any authority figure, he is someone to attack. Whatever the reaction, the group becomes aware of it. If he either overreacts or underreacts, he reduces the potential for learning.

Skill is needed in setting an example from the very start, without appearing to do so deliberately: an example of personal behavior, especially under criticism. But though he sets an example, he must make it clear that the lab members need not follow it and that they can reject his way of behaving, his kind of reactions, if they choose. His aim is to help them see themselves as they now are and experiment with ways of becoming the kinds of people they would like to be. All in all, his role is that of a catalyst. He is there to release and expedite candid and free communication among all the members of the group.

THE RATING TECHNIQUE

The conference leader may listen with some interest, though he is more likely observing the reactions of the members as shown by their posture, smoking, yawning, doodling, facial expressions. These may be discussed after the coffee break when the leader asks the group to rate the morning's meeting. He asks each man to write on a slip of paper, using "1" as the lowest score and "9" as the highest, his evaluation of how satisfied he is with this session. The papers are collected, the scores listed on the blackboard, and an average computed. It is generally fairly low, about "4." The leader may then ask the person who gave the lowest score to the morning meeting to explain the reasons for his rating. The same procedure may be followed with persons who rated the session with the highest score.

He may also help the members analyze and interpret their individual behavior. For example, in regard to the introductions, how much did anyone reveal about his real self? Who avoided all personal references? Whom do the trainees feel they now know best and whom the least? Were the men really introducing their companies and hiding themselves?

The rating system is used several times daily throughout the first week. The scores are kept on the board so that comparisons can be made. The ratings serve as a mirror of what the group sees as its own effectiveness. The feedback following each rating provides additional raw material from the men's own experiences for them to examine and study.

The sessions are interrupted daily for other kinds of ratings which will provide more data about the impact of the group members on each other. For example, they may be asked to rank other members. They are asked questions along these lines:

1. If you were selecting a business partner, which member of this group would be your first choice? Which member would be your last choice?
2. Which member of the group would you find it easiest to confide in? Which member would you find it most difficult to confide in?
3. If you wanted to go out socially with a member of this group, who would be your first choice? Who would be your last choice?

The answers are then posted on the blackboard. Each man knows how he looks to the others whom he is ranking. The rankings continue and are recorded daily. Thus a member can see what progress he has made in his relationships with others. Most important—everyone must give the reasons for his rankings.

Ken, say, may be rated the last choice as a confidant or the most difficult to talk to. If so, the leader asks those who scored Ken the lowest in these categories to tell why, and the reasons can be shocking. Ken may find them hard to believe. The discussion that follows may be heated and intense. Ken, the last choice for a partner? Why? Frank, the easiest to talk to? Why?

In stating their first choice as a business partner, five group members choose George. Why? George has been a sort of dark horse. At the start he seemed almost too good-natured and easy-going to be a top executive. What qualities emerged that led to his choice? What was his hidden strength?

One member sums it up, and the others agree. "He bends, but you have a feeling he wouldn't break."

Says another, "I think he'd know how to handle himself in the clinches. I didn't think so at first, but I do now. I think he knows how to roll with the punch, and he'd be a hell of a counter fighter. I like him, but I wouldn't want to cross him or push him too hard."

"If you get into an argument with George," a member explains, "he listens. He just sits back, looks interested, and lets you talk. And while he listens, with that good-natured smile on his face, you can see his mind is going click, click, click; but you feel it's an open mind. He's summing up all your arguments, and when you've had your say, he lets you have them back, along with his own reasons why he agrees or disagrees. But he listens."

Again: "I think George could win an argument in a country store. He won't give in if he feels he is right, but he won't shove it down your throat either. He doesn't need the help of a paneled office with a thick carpet and three telephones and two secretaries. Drop him anywhere, and he'll work well with people. I don't mind admitting that I'd like to copy his style."

Ratings and discussions often indicate that it's the member who needs the training the least who will probably get the most out of the meetings. But this is true of all kinds of emotional learning.

Most of us have unconscious defenses against criticism. It is too easy to feel that anyone who criticizes us is wrong. Unconscious fears create blind spots. The lab training, the feedback, the ratings, help remove the blind spots and help each member to accept well-meant criticism, not in anger but with calm self-appraisal and eventual gratitude.

Group ratings will often cause a member to be profoundly moved. "I'm really stunned," one member says. "I honestly thought I was the kind of person everyone came to with his problems. Yet not one of you rates me as a person you'd want to confide in. It shakes me."

Another man speaks up. "It's revealing. I have to admit

it. I think of myself as a dynamic executive. Well informed. Well able to express opinions. But I never . . . honestly, I never thought of my manner as domineering. I didn't realize people think I talk too damned much, that I monopolize discussion, and that I brush off the opinions of others and never listen to views that I disagree with. But now as I look back, I can think of occasions when these things have probably been true."

Thus the T-group offers no mold for the trainee to fit into, no doctrine, no single formula. It says, "Open your eyes. Look at yourself. See how you look to others. Then decide what changes, if any, you want to make and in which direction you want to go."

THE END OF THE FIRST DAY

The end of the first day finds many of the T-group members frustrated and puzzled. While the purpose of lab training is clear, the process is confusing—especially the lack of structure and apparent lack of direction. A few of the men find this formlessness stimulating: they are challenged by the absence of an agenda and the lack of a planned program.

But the majority of the trainees are upset at this new approach and even hostile, although only a few may feel free as yet to express their hostility. Whatever their feelings, however, they are all aware that the unfreezing of old attitudes, old values, and old approaches has begun.

In most T-groups, the men are particularly struck by the contrast between the typical kind of staff meeting they are used to back home and the unstructured T-group session. In their own companies, one man dominates the typical meeting: *the boss*. He decides who is to be recognized and when discussion is to be cut off.

In the training lab, however, authority has shifted to the group. There the men must create their own agenda and decide how to proceed from their own alternatives. They find themselves under a kind of social microscope. They study themselves and the group and feed back their frank reactions and candid opinions of each other. The leader does not seem to lead at all.

By the time the Monday evening session is over, some men are frustrated, anxious, and tense. Others are puzzled but stimulated. They separate quickly into small groups and search for some form of recreation that will let them unwind. The bar is busiest this night. But this is the last evening the men will spend in this way. Twenty-four hours later the men are so deeply involved with themselves, each other, and the group that the T-group discussions continue far into the night.

CHAPTER IV

I'M A STRANGER HERE MYSELF •

To some extent we are all strangers. We are strangers to ourselves in the sense that we do not really understand our inner motives and feelings. We are strangers to each other because the image we project to the world outside is different from the way we see ourselves. We don't really know what we are like until we take off the masks we wear—masks we put on as much to fool others as to hide from ourselves.

In taking off the mask, we come to recognize the stranger within us. This is perhaps the greatest discovery a man makes in sensitivity training: in learning through feedback his real impact on other people, he begins to understand himself.

Let us take as an example a typical member of a T-group. Let us see how he affects the other members and they him and how, together, they begin to know each other and transform themselves from a collection of individuals into a cohesive group. The member called Ken is representative.

Ken has been president of his company for only a

short time. He has taken on his executive responsibility with a number of ideas about human relationships and human behavior that began to form when he was still a child. Some of these ideas came to him from his parents; others from his teachers and fellow pupils at school; still others from his buddies in the Navy where he served during World War II and from bosses under whom he worked and from whom he absorbed, more unconsciously than consciously, the image of the business leader he hoped to become one day.

Out of all of these, Ken developed a system of beliefs about people and how to deal with them that might be described as in accord with the traditional authority-obedience theory of management. He sees it as the duty of the boss to control and decide and of the subordinate to do what the boss tells him to do.

This is the system Ken brought to his job as president. He knew, of course, that he would be confronted with many problems at the start. But he was sure that he would be able to solve them. His record made him confident of both the soundness of his judgment and the range of his ability. The new job had some new requirements: it was not enough for the man who held it to be a practical administrator; he also had to have the ability to devise innovations, to create and make changes for the better. But Ken was sure that he could do these things. He was a tireless worker who was in the habit of devoting evenings and week ends to company problems. He was zealous in studying reports and proud of his ability to make decisions promptly, surely, and effectively. From a human relations seminar he had attended, Ken had brought back a simple formula to guide him in his relations with his subordinates: "Be firm, be fair, be friendly." Ken acted this way —so far as he knew.

But after some months on the job, Ken still wasn't getting the results he expected of himself and the stockholders expected of him. His biggest trouble seemed to be getting his management team to *move;* most of the bad habits they had acquired before Ken took over were still hampering their performance—and, eventually, Ken's. He found himself wondering whether there might not be something wrong with his idea of how to get the best efforts from his employees. They weren't bringing in the results expected. Something was missing—the kind of cooperative relationship with his men and the kind of company morale that turn a group of individuals into a hard-hitting team.

Ken made a surprising discovery: his dependence on other people was greater than ever, which he had not expected. Ken had always regarded the presidency as the position offering the greatest amount of independence.

As the problems piled up, Ken began to feel anxious and unhappy. Why didn't his staff identify more with the goals of the company? In what way had he failed to win and hold the loyalty of his subordinates? What could he do to make them function as a team?

Each employee, as he saw it, did his job, but he performed as an isolated "I" and not as a member of the team "we." Could their attitudes be changed? Could he and his subordinates work together like partners and not as mere hired hands working to get the most for the least?

Whatever he did to be "firm, fair, and friendly" was somehow failing to work out. Worse, several of the company's top executives resigned to take other jobs or go into business for themselves. Ken concluded that he needed to form a new executive team and to build it on terms different from those he had been relying on. He proposed to build this team around the personality of the company vice president, whose competency and loyalty he had above all relied on. But before he could launch this new reorganization, Ken received a personal letter from his vice president in which the man offered his resignation. In part, the letter said:

> Ken, I went through an emotional experience last night, and it was most disturbing. No one thing brought it on. I suddenly found myself wondering why I keep working nights as I do. My wife keeps calling me to come home. I say I still have work to do. When I finally get home, it's ten o'clock and I'm dog tired. Dinner is still hot, but I don't enjoy it, don't seem to care whether I eat or not.

> I'm worried, I mean, about the whole situation. Why do I work so hard? For what and above all for whom? I tell myself it's my job, that I have to do it. But that's not true. Nobody would fire me. I tell my wife it's to make more money, or that I want to get promoted. But when I think it over, I know these aren't the real reasons either.

> For the first time it occurred to me why I was doing so much work. It was to please you—to satisfy you, your plans, your needs—not mine.

> I thought, "Where do I come in?" I asked myself if I was going to go on working nights, as you do, for the rest of my life. What's so important in meeting your needs that makes me ignore my own?

> You're tough and you want results. I have no quarrel with that. But you have blind spots that keep you from getting close to people and their work problems, keep you from seeing the human side.

> You make all the important decisions yourself. Should you? I wonder. You pride yourself on being frank, blunt—on calling them as you see them. But what do you really see? You

are so skillful about getting your own way. I wonder if you realize that you sometimes jam your own ideas down other people's throats and make them agree with you.

You tell everyone what you think—oh, yes! Forcefully and emphatically, And what you think is that anyone who argues with you is soft or lacks ability or imagination. Or maybe that's just what you want us to think.

Maybe there's a reason for this deep need of yours to control everyone and everything. Could it be that you aren't as sure of yourself as you want to be, or as you think you are?

Maybe I'm not either. Maybe I have some of your faults. But if I have them I at least want to know about them, I want to find out. I'll never know as long as I work for you. I'm convinced of that.

So for this reason—and with no personal hard feelings, Ken —please consider this my resignation. I want it to take effect immediately.

For a long time after Ken read that letter, he just sat staring at it. It was signed, "Sincerely, Louis," and it was in his familiar handwriting, but it was hard to believe Louis had written it.

That letter was the payoff. Coming as it did on top of all his other problems in dealing with people, it convinced Ken that some sort of fundamental change was indicated. It was shortly afterward that his inquiries brought him to the training lab.

Here he discovers that life at the top was not always so complicated as it is now—that there was a time when the relationship of the boss to the employee was a simple straightforward affair: the lines of authority were direct and the channels of communication simple. The boss gave an order, and it was carried out—or else. Ken also learns why that kind of authoritarian boss is no longer as effective, no longer as suited to high-level management in a modern organization.

The T-group leader is explaining these matters to Ken:

In the old type of firm, there was a single source of authority, the chief executive. He was it. All final decisions went to him and came from him. We refer to it as the authority-obedience system.

The way he had matters controlled, there was supposed to be no room for error: the controls were tight. Instruction came straight from the top down. Every man had his boss; every supervisor, his supervisor. Even key executives had little or no authority to exercise personal judgment or in any smallest way to change the system.

In this type of firm, the chain of command had a hierarchy that was universally recognized and universally applied. There were staff functions and there were line functions. Each had its special preserve. The limit of authority on each managerial level was clearly defined. It was based on certain principles of organization that were considered classic, that were written into textbooks and taught at university schools of business administration.

Obviously this had a natural appeal for executives of a certain temperament, especially top ones. They might have indignantly denied it, but they thought of the people who worked for them as they thought of the machines on the production floor.

So it was the responsibility of management, especially top management, to see that men did as they were told. Directives were not open for discussion; nor were official policies, even old ones, subject to debate. The means of management control was authority, characterized by a unity of command much like the authority of a military machine.

The fact that the system seemed to work effectively in

military organizations and in the church, the two sources from which it was derived, gave these classic principles of organization a certain seal of approval.

Where it floundered, however, was in its inability to cope with the vast changes that were taking place in modern society: changes in education, changes in living standards, changes in technology. All of these were making vulnerable the traditional theories of business organization.

Perhaps the most significant change of all concerned the threat of dismissal. This had been industry's equivalent of the military court martial and of church excommunication. Its use as an ultimate control device was becoming so limited that it was of comparatively little consequence.

Ken listens avidly to this explanation. His expression, however, indicates he does not agree with much of what he hears.

"Many companies," says the group leader, "still operate on organizational practices that run counter to what we know about human behavior. They were successful in the past; but like it or not, they'll have to start applying scientific knowledge about human nature and managerial practices if they want to stay on top. Many companies are aware of this; others are changing and showing improvement."

"Like what, for instance?" Ken ask grudgingly. Observing his reaction, one gets the feeling he wants to know the answer but is afraid of what he might hear.

"Like giving people a feeling of achievement in their work, an opportunity as group members to participate in making decisions, and a chance to satisfy their need for recognition. They need exactly what you yourself need when you've done something really well. It raises your self-respect. It gives you something to be proud about—in your own eyes and in those of colleagues and friends. Every person has to feel a purpose and meaning to his life."

When Ken speaks, his voice, like his expression, betrays his impatience. "I honestly can't see that these things are any concern of top management. I have 10,000 employees. Am I expected to add their need for self-esteem to my other responsibilities? I don't think the experience of the past has proved that management has any obligation to be concerned with anything more than production, wages, benefits, and the like. All right, it's the past. But we can't just brush off past experience, especially when we've built the world's greatest industrial economy."

The group leader refrains from taking up the challenge, waiting for someone else to speak. The one who does is Ted. He and Ken did some talking the night before over a highball. They liked each other, although their personalities were quite different. Perhaps that was why Ted feels freer than some of the others to be frank with Ken.

"Ken," Ted says, "you were talking last night about a human relations course you took years ago and about a kind of slogan you remembered, one that still impressed you. I think it was, 'Be fair, be firm, be friendly.' Was that it?"

Ken nods in agreement.

"The fact is," Ted continues, "you talk about being friendly, but—well, I wonder whether you really are. Toward your associates, I mean. You may want to, may think you are, but—you don't *look* friendly. Or *sound* it."

Ted smiles to soften his next remark. "You can say the word 'friendly' and make it sound like a command. I think you *want* to be friendly—but it doesn't come through. Is it because you've never learned how to show friendliness?"

A chuckle goes around the table. Ken looks a bit embarrassed, a bit annoyed, then he chuckles too. "Okay, lay it on. I came here to learn something, didn't I?"

Ted continues, "I can imagine how you sound when you say you want something done in your organization. 'Directive' would be too mild a word for it. It's an *order*, and I wouldn't want to question it, even if I had a good reason to. You're firm, all right, the way you see it. Your staff probably sees it as being bullheaded. Whether you're always fair is something else. You may think you are, but there must be times when you appear to them just the opposite. The point is that you'll never know—and that's where the trouble lies. Come to think of it, though, maybe you don't *want* to know."

"Sure I want to know," Ken interrupts. "I can take it— I had to learn how as a kid. I grew up in a tough neighborhood, and I learned to handle myself. I grew up the hard way, and I . . ."

"I suppose you'll be telling us next that you had an unhappy childhood," Ted interrupts to say. "So did we all. Everybody in this room had an unhappy childhood. So quit feeling sorry for yourself. We can all write pages about the unhappy events in our growing-up years—kids on the street who beat us up, teachers and schools that made life miserable, strict parents who belted us too often. Sure, some had it tougher than others, but kids know only their own experiences and don't know the difference." Ted pauses to see how he is registering.

"Go ahead," Ken says. "I'm still listening."

"Okay, Ken, then here it is," Ted continues. "I think a lot of good men wouldn't want to work for you. I know I wouldn't. And do you know why? For one thing, because I won't take orders the way you give them. As Steve said a little while ago, the kind of attitude you expressed and the things you were telling me last night probably work fine in the military, but we're all civilians now, and a lot of people—particularly the good ones—are simply not going to take it."

Ted pauses again, this time for emphasis. "I have a hunch some good men have quit your organization, Ken. If they haven't, they're liable to."

While Ted's comments—particularly the last one—are sinking in, another group member, Henry, has a more constructive comment for Ken. "If Ken's having a difficult management problem, perhaps I can make a suggestion."

"Glad to hear it," says Ken.

Henry says that Ken sounds as if he is unfamiliar with "participative" management. Ken admits he doesn't know much about it, although he has heard about this type of management. By this time, however, Ken is ready to listen with more than grudging attention as Henry speaks of the way participative management practices have built a team of managers in his company who can work cooperatively on solving problems, setting goals, and building a more effective organization.

"I think," Henry concludes, "you could get some real improvement in the use of human resources if you gave your team the authority to plan together, work on specific solutions, and make some group decisions. I think you'd get cooperation—and I think it would last—especially if you introduced a managerial approach where you collaborated with your staff instead of just commanding them. This might mean a major change in management practices; and there would be problems of authority and delegation, of reconciling differences, and of rearranging the patterns of influence."

The leader picks up the discussion. He speaks about findings in the behavioral sciences: psychology, sociology, anthropology—and of the work of men such as Rensis

Likert, Chris Argyris, Douglas McGregor, and Warren Bennis to the effect that management's traditional assumptions about human nature are often rationalizations which are meant to explain away operating troubles by blaming the employees instead of management. He gives examples of such rationalizations:

1. People inherently dislike work and for this reason must be closely supervised.
2. Most people are selfish, show little ambition, and have a fear of responsibility.
3. People respond most to pressure, are dependent, want to be told what to do, and like to avoid making decisions.
4. People always take advantage; try to get something for nothing; and if you give them an inch, take a mile.
5. Dog eat dog is the rule of the universe, and the only way to get along is to be tougher and stronger and to hit first.

"If there's any truth in these statements," the leader suggests, "and I don't say they're not without a grain of truth, it could be the result of managerial practices that are contrary to our present knowledge about the human needs of people in the work relationships.

"Any system set up to control people as though they were irresponsible, self-centered, and indifferent—and must be so treated by the few who are responsible—is likely to encourage them to behave that way. You fit them into the system if you have the power to do so—and managers do have the power. Then, when people behave as they have been compelled to, you insist they were born that way and can't behave in any other way.

"Management's troubles with high turnover, absenteeism, low productivity, featherbedding practices, strikes, poor quality, and other inadequacies that contribute to higher costs—all these are the result of the failure to deal competently with the human needs of employees and of false assumptions about human nature."

The leader cites the results of a survey made by the Survey Research Center of the University of Michigan. Its purpose was to find out why people work. Questions were put to people all over the country—hourly wage earners, salaried executives, and professional men. In all three groups, an overwhelming majority answered that they worked not because they had to, but because they wanted to. Asked if they would continue to work if they were assured enough income to satisfy all their needs for the rest of their lives, 80 per cent in all three groups said yes. But when it came to attitudes toward their jobs, there was a significant difference between the answers of the hourly workers and the answers of the professional groups. The vast majority of hourly workers stated they would not want to stay at the same job. But almost all of the physicians, lawyers, accountants, and other professionals answered that they would want to continue in the same work.

Those around the table in the T-group agree that the express desire to continue working indicates that working fills an important need of the adult in our society.

"Now then," the group leader continues, "let's talk about the broader implications of this problem. Why do people work at all? The facts seem to support the view that to most people, work is a source of fulfillment, not a penance.

"The cliché that man works for bread alone is true when he has no bread. But when his physical needs—the primary requirements of food and shelter—are met, the higher psychological needs demand to be satisfied. Call them what you like: ego satisfactions, self-esteem, or simply 'pride.' By any name, these needs are real. They are keenly felt. They are important.

"But are they satisfied? Rarely, I would say, in an organization that operates with rigid controls, controls imposed from above with authority as the chief motivator."

"Remember," the leader says, "most of the professionals in the survey were satisfied to continue with what they were doing. These men had some degree of independence and control over their actions. Most of the wage earners had little opportunity to determine their own activities and not much chance to show what they could do without being controlled. They wanted to try something else for a change.

"Self-esteem—and a feeling of human dignity—these are at the very core of our emotional life; and a vital part of this self-esteem comes from the feeling that we are self-directing—that we have some voice in controlling the things that matter in our own life. Any damage to this view of self can be as painful as actual physical harm. More so, in fact. And any system or organization that causes this harm, that detracts from self-esteem, is going to cause open or smouldering resentment.

"In many companies today there is a growing awareness of the human side of enterprise, of the interdependence of employee and employer—a growing recognition that sanctions could be applied in both directions and that it is therefore imperative that the relationship between employee and employer become a two-way street."

Frank speaks next. He is from a company that has had some experience with decentralization and wide delegation of the authority to make decisions.

"Let me assure you that there was nothing soft or sentimental about our decision to decentralize," he says. "Sure it was different. It threw the men more on their own resources. Did that make it easier? No, harder, if anything. Yet they liked it. And it paid off for us, for the firm.

Especially when the men began to get the idea that what was good for the company was good for them.

"Did we get different levels of management together? Sure we did. Were we able to promote group effort? Of course. Did that mean the production worker had a voice in my decisions? Obviously not. But it did mean that I had to make a lot fewer of his decisions. And believe me, that's much better for both of us."

"I'd like to know," says Joe, "if you believe all companies can benefit from participative management. I'd also like to know why you are willing to give up the power of being boss—a goal you devoted your life to attaining."

Frank answers, "Not only do I think every company can benefit, but I am convinced that this is the only way companies will be run during the years to come. In our own organization we have seen all kinds of improvements. Man-hour production is higher. Turnover is lower. There are fewer controls; yet quality control has been maintained. And this may come as something of a surprise: employee take-home pay is higher, while our per-unit cost is lower! Yet I have more power, not the power of control but of growth."

At this point, Ken speaks up again. He is still being hardheaded. "All I know is that any time I was in charge of a department and made innovations, I met with resistance from my subordinates. You think they wanted to participate? Did they want to change from the way they'd been doing things? They did not. They said that the old way was better. The new way would never work. They wanted to keep on doing their work the same way. How are you going to get people like that to assume responsibility, to participate, to share in the decision-making process? They'll fight every change, every advance, every progressive move and prove to you why it won't work."

Ken gets his answer, in a roundabout way, from another member, Jerry, who says, "I just know about my own company and my own people. When I think how rough competition is these days, it seems to me I've got to look to every employee in the place—not just the key executives —to come up with new ideas to save money, new ways of operating to increase efficiency, even new products to make and new ways to sell them.

"As for you, Ken, maybe if your staff didn't feel so dependent, they'd be a little less hesitant about trying out a new idea. Remember when your employees resist your innovations that this might be one way they have of expressing dissatisfaction. Remember, too, that people don't learn to become independent by being kept dependent. You have to think in terms of a long-range program. There is no magic system you can introduce and get results overnight.

"I get the impression you're not easy to satisfy. Maybe your people are afraid they won't do it right or won't get things exactly as you want them. If they were given a little more freedom and responsibility, maybe they'd be more receptive to new ideas."

Into the silence that follows comes a somewhat hesitant, low-pitched voice the T-group has rarely heard since the meetings had started. This is Dave, who speaks with a soft accent and an almost diffident manner.

"You fellows have been talking about satisfied employees. It seems to me that a satisfied employee is a productive employee. Does that jibe with your experience as it does with mine?"

The T-group listens more out of surprise than politeness: Dave is not one whom the lab members expected to hear more from, since his participation has been minimal up to this point.

"I have a feeling that some of you, at least," Dave continues, "think participative management is a kind of 'happiness boys approach,' a form of tranquilizer for the employees used to keep them content with their lot or maybe even make them feel a little better. It's nothing like that. It's different, but it is businesslike; and it's about time most companies recognized that times have changed and that the chain of command should now be a circle instead of a straight line from the top down."

Henry speaks for the group. "I think what you say makes sense, Dave. And, by the way, welcome to the group. We were kind of wondering when you'd care to join us. I'm glad you did. But are you this silent in your company? And how do your people see your reluctance to participate?"

"I've got some questions of my own," Henry continues. "I want to know what I can do to develop a real commitment to company goals by my employees. How can I get them to think in terms of 'we'? How can I motivate them, get them to feel they're really part of the company team?"

Frank has a quick reply: "First thing you have to do is stop using that first-person singular so often. You ask, 'How can *I* do it?' Maybe you ought to get into the habit of saying 'we.' If you say it often enough, you may even get to thinking that way. I think you should look into your own motivation. It might help you learn how to motivate others. But as long as you're talking and thinking in terms of the 'I,' they're not going to bother about the 'we.' "

Frank turns the pages of a notebook. "Here's what Douglas McGregor says. He's referring to his Theory Y of management. 'Management is basically an affair of teaching and training, not of directing and controlling. We control the process, not the people.' "

A few minutes later, Bob turns the discussion to the role of home and school in developing a different attitude in young people about their job expectations. "I have two boys, and they are typical, I think. They are encouraged to participate fully in matters that affect them in school and at home, ranging from the kind of car the family should buy to where the family should go for its vacation. In their daily activities, youngsters are given greater freedom today and encouraged to exercise more initiative and to develop more self-direction than I ever knew. There is a whole generation of youngsters who are being raised like this today—kids who are going to expect similar opportunities to share in solving problems when they start working."

"I think a lot depends on the way people react to authority," Joe interrupts to say. "Some rebel against it and fight any boss. Others are dependent and like to lean on someone. But I think the way our youngsters are being raised today isn't going to make it easy for them if they have the bad luck to get a job with a company that operates on strong controls imposed from above. They didn't have it at home, and they won't accept it on the job."

To which the leader adds, "Any business which depersonalizes its employees creates a problem for itself which will show up in its productivity and growth. This is why the progressive company today, as never before, must concern itself with the needs of its personnel and seek to improve interpersonal relations—not for reasons of philanthropy but for the sake of profits."

He continues, "The complaint that employees will do the least they can get away with in return for their wages is probably justified in the authoritarian type of organization. There the company gets the least rather than the most from its workers. The employees demand all the traffic will bear and give as little as possible in return. Such companies can be identified by the following:

1. A formal structure.
2. Supervisors who exert pressure on those immediately below them.
3. A system of autocratic controls via budgets and other devices that circumscribe the individual's freedom of decision and lead to a kind of behavior that parallels in effect the hamstringing of company executives by government controls."

The hour is late, and the group agrees to call it a day, but the men continue talking about McGregor and participative management, a not-unusual occurrence in sensitivity training. Afternoon discussions have a way of going on until it's time to assemble again for the evening. Evening sessions often go on till midnight.

When Steve's T-group finally turns in late that night, most of the men are ready to concede that in spite of the fact that participative management means giving up some measure of influence and control, there is something far greater to be gained and that from the standpoint of company profits (let alone what the men might derive from it) management gets the best deal from participative management. The men in the group have shown they are ready to begin the process of unfreezing some of their old values and of learning a little about their impact on each other.

CHAPTER V

A CHANGE OF PACE •

A WEDNESDAY MORNING in a training lab might start something like this. It is 8:00 A.M. and the trainees are finishing breakfast. Frank sits back, lights a cigar, and says he's glad the day is going to start with a general or theory session.

"That meeting in my room last night didn't break up until 2:00 A.M. It's enough to make a fellow groggy. And that unstructured business yesterday was enough to make anyone dizzy."

"Oh, I stayed up too," Ed replies, "but by the time we got through talking over our problems and reactions to each other, I was all wound up. I was awake half the night thinking about it."

If Frank is looking forward to finding a quiet corner

to catch forty winks during the theory session, he will probably be disappointed, for these sessions, attended by all
50 or 60 trainees together, provide a refreshing and yet
stimulating break from the introspection and feedback of
the ten-man T-groups. They serve to provide answers to
questions the men have been raising about the purpose of
the laboratory experiences and how they differ from the
usual training programs in human relations.

A general or theory session may begin with a discussion
of so-called human relations training. Such training assumes that a person's behavior can be satisfactorily altered
by means of lectures and reading. But attitudes don't
change that easily, and courses made up of lectures and
readings in human relations do little to produce results on
the job.

Merely being told to be patient or firm is of insufficient
help in solving an actual problem. If, for example, a purchasing agent has overinventoried, a salesman's account is
overdrawn, or a customer's bill is past due, what is the
approximate mix of patience and firmness that the boss
should use to get the man in question to (1) solve the
problem and (2) not make the same mistake the next
time? How can the subordinate be made to learn? Because
so many of these problems involve emotional elements and
deeply rooted assumptions about the self, a different kind
of learning experience is needed—one that gives the executive a deeper awareness of the impact he has on others.

Lectures may enlarge a man's vocabulary and broaden
his understanding, but they do all too little to change his
behavior. Principles and techniques may be memorized
faithfully, but applying them in a way that gets improved
results is something else. The need for a new way to learn
that links knowledge and conduct is obvious.

Thus the conference leader in his presentation at the

theory session points out that learning about human relations requires a different approach from learning dentistry or engineering, for example. In studying such technical subjects, the student does not begin with his own strong pre-conceptions of the principles to be learned.

Dealing with attitudes is a different matter. Each of us brings to the study of human relations his own life experiences, his own ideas about what makes people tick, his own habitual ways of dealing with and responding to friends, family, colleagues.

To learn about people—ourselves and others—a kind of confrontation with psychic realities is needed, such as that provided by the T-group's reaction to a member's behavior as expressed in the feedback and rating-scale processes characteristic of the human relations training lab, for it is the manner in which experience is introduced and acquired that is the decisive factor in producing a real change in attitudes and habitual ways of acting.

Facts become useful and fall into place only when the individual himself is reoriented in his search for a new solution. Through a process of guided experiences, the participant becomes aware of and then gradually comes to accept the attitude changes which he needs for greater personal effectiveness—changes he is able to practice in the lab.

"So it is obvious," the group leader says, "that only a kind of training that enables a person to see the impact of his behavior on others while it encourages him to learn new and better ways of dealing with people is likely to have a lasting effect. Basic to both of these goals is the process of self-examination. Without such a self-examination the man with 25 years' experience is really only a person with one year's experience repeated 25 times. The T-group provides a learning experience by which the participant reappraises and examines his basic attitudes and values in regard to other people. The training laboratory is the stage on which he acts these attitudes out and tests for audience reaction.

SKILL SESSION IN ROLE PLAYING

After a brief question period, the theory session concludes. When the T-group reassembles, the leader may explain that another group will join them for a role-playing session. When the second group is seated, the leader talks about role playing, describing it as another kind of learning procedure.

Getting along cooperatively with people requires specific social skills, and like other skills these can be learned and perfected. There is only one effective way to acquire these skills: practice them, watch others practice them, discuss them and their actual impact on others, and try again.

Role playing has the advantage of showing forcefully how something is most effectively done rather than telling how it is done. We all recognize the difference between the fellow who "talks a good game" and the one who can really perform. In role playing, practice sessions are set up as substitutes for life experiences. By acting out everyday problems it becomes possible to play for fun before playing for keeps.

Problems can be role-played with as few as two or as many as ten. In a T-group, the participants analyze and interpret the role play and share with each other their reactions to each of the players on the others. For example, in one standard exercise, two trainees may be given the roles of two executives. One may take the part of an assistant, and the other may play his boss. The theme is why the assistant hasn't been given the promotion he feels he deserves. Or a whole T-group may become a "department" and act out some problem.

There is no script: the problem and the part each is to play are merely sketched out. There is no rehearsal: the characters act out their roles spontaneously—and in terms of their own personal notion of how the problem should be handled.

One advantage of role playing is that it provides the opportunity to practice lifelike situations without real-life risks. It allows trainees in lab training to experiment safely with managerial approaches that are different from their usual style. Emphasis is placed on the kind of situations a man is likely to face on a typical day back on the job.

Through the use of a variety of role-playing episodes, a group can observe several different approaches to every-day executive problems and consider various solutions. And at the same time a member may learn, from the group's reaction to his own approach, about the strength or weakness of his own managerial style.

In every company, situations arise in which the managers have different points of view on how to handle some serious issue. Yet all must be satisfied or at least willing to accept the solution if they are to continue to work together cooperatively. The task of the manager is to learn how to meet this kind of situation so that the best solution is agreed upon rather than the solution advocated by the most vocal members or by the smoothest salesmen. It is essential, from the company point of view, that the best solution be adopted even if it involves conflict. How to deal with such issues is a typical role-play problem.

If several members of the group are going to play the same role in later reruns of the same problem—that is, are going to be given the same problem to handle—all except the first "actors" are asked to leave the room, to be called back one at a time. In this way, no one acting the part later will know in advance how others have met the problem.

One instructive role-play session that brings two T-groups together calls for five volunteers to play the part of workers in a conflict situation and three men to act as supervisors, each separately trying to resolve the conflict in his own way. The remaining 12 men are members of the audience. They observe and analyze the way the problem is handled by the three "supervisors" in turn and compare each one's performance with what they would have done themselves. They also observe how the workers behave: who is ready to compromise, who will fight to the finish, who shows feeling for the other fellow, who is seemingly concerned only for himself.

The group leader explains: "This isn't the kind of problem that would be likely to face a man on your management level. It's simpler, on the whole, but it will disclose more clearly how leadership varies in style, how each man has his own way of dealing with the same situation."

He announces that five men are to play the roles of parcel-delivery truckdrivers. Each of them has a valid reason, or feels he has, for demanding the one new truck which the manager is to assign. Each of the five executives-turned-truckdriver is given the special reason why he should be entitled to the new truck.

"Try to keep it in character," the leader says. "Forget that you were ever a manager. For the moment be a truckdriver. In this situation you're taking care of the only fellow who counts, as far as you're concerned. That's you. Never mind the supervisor's problem. That's *his* headache. You've got one of your own."

He points to one volunteer. "You're Joe. You have

top seniority. Naturally you expect the truck to be assigned to you."

He points to another. "You're Bill. You have the oldest truck. You take for granted they'll replace it with the new one."

And to another. "You're Mack. You put more mileage into your truck than any of the others. It's only reasonable, you feel, that you should have the new one."

And to the fourth. "You're Jack. You claim to cover almost as many miles as Mack. But you have another beef. There was an accident with your truck, and it was never properly repaired. There's a crack in the cab door, next to the driver's seat. It lets in a lot of cold air. That's bad, especially for you, a veteran with a bum leg."

Finally, to the fifth. "You're Harry. You're second in seniority. You're right next to Joe. But Joe got the last new truck, not quite two years ago. You're next in line, so you feel it's your turn for a new one."

Then the group leader picks the first of the "supervisors" to begin the role-playing exercise and asks the other two to leave the room. Jerry, the first supervisor, is direct. He doesn't waste time. He gets the five drivers together and explains the situation.

"We have a new truck, fellows. Just one. I can't give it to all of you, and I want to be open about it so there won't be any grumbling later. Joe, here, has seniority, and I go by the book. The new truck is going to Joe. I don't want to hear any arguments. That's all. Let's get moving on the routes."

The next supervisor is called in. His method is quite different. He makes the announcement about the truck; then he listens and lets each man give his reasons for needing it. Finally, he says, "You've all got good reasons, and any decision I might make would look as though I were favoring one of you. I don't want that. I have to live with you guys every day. So I'm going to turn it over to the personnel department. Let them decide. That way you can be sure at least that you're getting an unbiased decision."

Then the third supervisor acts out his role. He also listens to all five drivers. Then he says: "Now look. You fellows all think you're right. No matter whom I give the truck to, nobody's going to think I'm fair except the man who gets it. I want you fellows to get together and work something out for yourselves."

There's some grumbling about this at first. "He's supposed to be a supervisor. *Anybody* can pass the buck." But they start to work the problem out, and within 15 minutes they have arrived at a solution—some with more enthusiasm than others. They agree, first, that no matter who gets the truck, each driver's situation will be improved. What does it is a suggestion by one of the five truckdrivers that they get rid of the old truck before assigning the new one. Once the men decide which truck is to go, a rather complicated shifting around follows, as a result of which each man gets a different truck to drive. The man who ranks second in seniority gets the new one. In the end, the five truckdrivers are rather pleased with their problem-solving skill.

When the role-playing incident is finished, the 12 observers ask questions and make comments. All note how much the supervisors' solutions differed from each other, and the discussion centers around managerial capability and supervisory competence. Many questions are asked:
- Would you have handled it differently?
- Which supervisor was most likely to be respected by his men for the way he handled the situation?
- Would the men feel more cooperative because the solu-

tion was their own and was not imposed upon them?
* Suppose the same solution had been developed by the supervisor without consulting the men. Would they have accepted it?

The discussion then shifts to observations of the drivers' behavior: who created conflict, who offered to compromise, who tried to dominate, whether the solution was a good one for the company, whether it was the best one for the men, and whether the atmosphere was one of winners and losers or pleasant and friendly team action.

The leader sums up as follows:

> The three different patterns of leadership you observed may be called the autocratic, the evasive, and the participative. The three types of leaders are the "dominator," the "compromiser," and the "harmonizer."

> It will be valuable to examine these three styles of leadership. Let's draw a profile of each, blocking out the character line expressive of the behavior of each type.

THREE STYLES OF LEADERSHIP

The *dominator* sees himself as a blunt, no-nonsense boss. His job is to make the decisions for those under him. Since the discipline he imposes on his subordinates is matched by his own obedience, he considers himself to be a strong advocate of "company teamwork." "Teamwork" is a word he often uses.

He fancies himself a put-up-or-shut-up type. Compromise annoys him. He looks bored if you talk about the "human side of management." Privately, he believes in the rule of the strong. The strong and able succeed. Others must take the consequences of their personal limitations. The authority-obedience system of management is the only one he respects.

"I call the shots as I see them," he'll tell anyone. "The human side? Sure I'm human. But that doesn't mean I'm going to mollycoddle the people who know me as the boss." He does not tolerate disagreements; and if conflict exists in his staff, it is usually kept under cover. He thinks participation in decisions means carrying them out, not help in making them.

He believes people who make mistakes should be punished quickly and with severity, that controls must be tight, and that other managers should constantly pressure those who work under them—just as he closely supervises his subordinates.

He makes the rules, criticizes violators, and personally tries to follow up on every aspect of operations. He is a great believer in systems and paperwork as controls on his employees. He does the planning and tells the others what must be done.

The *compromiser,* on the other hand, is sometimes considered an "easy boss" compared to the dominator. It is true that he doesn't want to push people. He says he doesn't believe in it. He wants to get good results, but without driving his men too hard. He thinks going for that last ounce only results in resentment and is not worth the price.

He often finds himself making accommodations out of a desire to avoid conflict, even though he may believe his position is the right one. He is a kind of juggler: he wants to get the job done, and he also wants people to be satisfied. He may want things to move at a faster pace but feels that if he keeps pushing he won't get the best results. He sees himself as a "practical" executive. That's one of *his* favorite words. But this is also his way of rationalizing his moderate accomplishments. He avoids setting high goals and takes a middle-of-the-road position. He overlooks mistakes if they don't occur too often. He does the planning but modifies his proposals if they are challenged. He has one thing in common with the dominator: he believes firmly in "teamwork."

The *harmonizer* also believes in teamwork. So it becomes a question of what the phrase means to each of the three. The harmonizer feels that consideration for those under him brings out their best. He feels it's important to understand the personal needs, the wants, the goals of his employees or his colleagues. He strives for excellence and aims at the highest results which are compatible with a genuine concern for people and their needs.

He would like his subordinates to enjoy their work. He believes that they will work better and produce more if they think well of the boss and like and respect him and if he does the same in return and lets them know it.

He expects there will be strong disagreements among his men, but he encourages them to find the areas of agreement. He helps them find points on which they can get together so that they can work for a further agreement. So instead of suppressing conflict, he gets all the people involved in it in order to work it through.

The harmonizer emphasizes participation. He keeps his employees informed and reviews common problems with them. Wherever possible, he brings his men into a new situation from the beginning, shares his plans with them, and encourages them to participate with him in solving problems and making decisions. Since he depends on mutual trust and confidence, he handles mistakes by developing corrective measures in conjunction with those who made the mistakes. Finally, he tries to bring out the warmth of human relationships. He is often on friendly terms with his men and enjoys their confidence. Sometimes when they have troubles, they will pay him the compliment of coming to him for advice.

"There is, of course, a little bit of each of these in every executive, although his overall behavior will put him in one of the three categories," the T-group leader explains. "I leave it to you to figure out where you think you fit in. Later, we'll compare how you rate yourself with the way the other members of the group see you as revealed by your behavior here. The results may be surprising—and educational. And they'll provide further opportunity for feedback."

CHAPTER VI

AS OTHERS SEE US •

ON THURSDAY MORNING the training leader proposes two exercises to the group.

"The first one," he says, "is a self-appraisal of your managerial style, which we have classified into three types: the dominator, the compromiser, and the harmonizer. Think over these classifications and select the one which you think most closely describes your managerial approach. Then look around the room and classify each of the other members of your group." He distributes paper, the trainees make their choices, and the sheets are collected without further comment.

Then the leader says, "Now for the second exercise. I would like each man to spend 30 minutes writing a description of the kind of person he thinks he is." When this has been done, he collects the papers and announces that he will read the descriptions to the group, who are to identify the authors from what they hear. The identifications are remarkably unsuccessful. They make it clear how rarely people see themselves as others see them.

"Bill, I don't know if this will offend you, but your description of yourself amazes me. You say you're really shy inside. You certainly don't act it. The outside just doesn't match. Seems to me you try to control and dominate every situation you come in contact with. You often speak in such an impatient tone that you give the impression you don't expect anybody to like what you're saying and that you couldn't care less whether they like it or not."

"Ralph, you baffle me. What's this about the 'compassion' you say you feel? You haven't really warmed up to anybody yet. If you have these warm feelings, why do they have to be kept so deeply inside of you? When the talk gets around to matters of emotion or feeling, you clam up or shift the conversation to a more general topic. You do! I've noticed it. Why do you hide the inner man, Ralph? Why not reveal him? What are you afraid of?"

"You wrote that you don't aim to win any popularity contests, Ken. I wonder if you're so right about that. Oh, you *act* as though you don't give a damn what others think of you—most of the time, that is. But I often get the feeling you really hope people are going to like you, in spite of your attitude. And you say you're the kind of person who says what's on his mind, even if you think nobody will agree with you. But you know, Ken, this may surprise you, but I don't believe you're really expressing what's really on your mind. I think you expect people to disagree with you, and so you try to live up to their expectations by saying things that will rile them up."

After these comments are made, the leader writes the results of the first exercise on the blackboard. The group members are astounded by what they read. Of the four who saw themselves as harmonizers, only one is so rated by his fellow trainees. Of the three who described themselves as dominators, only two are accepted as such. The three men who called themselves compromisers are classified by the group as dominators.

"The results," says the leader, "are evidence of a serious but common failure to see ourselves as others do." Several of the members raise questions about these blind spots, and all agree to explore the problem further.

The first question raised concerns perception. To answer the question, the group leader quotes the noted psychologist Dr. Hadley Cantril, who made use of a story of three baseball umpires in order to make clear how differently perception may be understood.

The first umpire says, "Some's balls and some's strikes. I call 'em as they are."

The second says, "Some's balls and some's strikes. I call 'em as I see 'em."

The third says, "Some may be balls and some may be strikes, but they ain't nothing until I call 'em."

The leader then goes on to explain as follows:

> Don't all our perceptions fit into these three molds? A few facts may be unequivocal, the same for everybody who sees them. We call 'em as they are. Other facts require conscious interpretation. We call them as we see them. But most of our so-called facts—the ones upon which a company executive bases his decisions—are filtered, manipulated, and modified. It is his unconscious that censors and edits them. They "ain't nothing until he calls 'em," and the company's well-being depends on them. Actually, what his eye sees is shaped by his "I," and different "I's" make different shapes for the eye.

> Often we see facts—particularly the vital facts about a situation in which we're emotionally involved—not as *they* really are but as *we* are.

Some perceptions that we ignore are carefully noted by others. Some make a profound impression on us; others we don't notice. A mother sleeps soundly despite loud noises from the street, but she wakes instantly when her baby whimpers.

Seen in this light, the executive's standard bromide—"Let's look at the facts"—must also entail a look inside the viewer. The equally ancient adage, "Seeing is believing," may turn out to be more accurate when it is repeated backward: "Believing is seeing." Often—too often—it is the belief that is established first. Then we perceive only those situations which agree with our beliefs. A manager who believes that people are lazy and shirk responsibility does not "see" people who behave contrary to his beliefs. The facts that threaten his established beliefs are not seen—they become blind spots.

It is this aspect of perception—seeing more through the "I" than the "eye"—that so frequently causes conflict within a business organization.

A production chief makes decisions based on plant output. These are the facts as he sees them. But working with the same data his counterparts in sales or finance may suggest other decisions. Their "I's" build facts in different ways. Facts to the production manager may be fiction to the others. What a purchasing agent sees as a conservative way of building inventory may appear radical to a controller.

How, then, can we learn to recognize the difference between what really is and what we add to our perceptions of ourselves, others, places, and things? Obviously the one thing we can do is compare the way we see ourselves, see other people, and see the facts themselves as we've been doing here. The naked truth is *not* indecent exposure—as some of you may have felt this week. It calls for confronting oneself without fear and without prejudice, for exposing ourselves truly and wholly to the eyes of others as well as to our own eyes.

Now, as for this self-image, how did it develop? Where did it come from? It is, of course, largely an unconscious process, one that begins early in life and is patterned originally on the parental image. And as the individual matures, the self-image tends to reflect not only the qualities he actually possesses but those idealized qualities he wants others to believe he possesses.

Thus is the idealized self-image developed. And once it is developed, what happens then? Well, it has to be defended, doesn't it? Defended against reality. And so the self-image becomes the object of a number of defensive and enhancement tactics adopted to protect ourselves from hurt to our pride, criticism of our behavior, doubt, uncertainty, and fear. Two of the most common of these tactics are *regression* and *rationalization*.

What is regression? It can be described as an unconscious return to childlike behavior in meeting difficulties. For example, a boss shouts at his secretary and reduces her to tears, which he then calls "childish." But how does he look to her? Shouting, carrying on? Doesn't *he* look childish?

Probably the most common of *all* defense techniques is rationalization, the finding of *good* reasons rather than *real* reasons for our conduct. The rationalizer finds excuses for those actions which might otherwise seem undesirable.

There is no shortage of examples, for we are all adept at rationalizing our failures. A salesman is criticized for falling behind last year's figures. Perhaps he failed to adapt to changes in the line, to explore a newly opened market, or to meet his competition as aggressively as did other salesmen in the company. But he does not look for the real reasons for his failure. Instead he argues, "I could be the top salesman in the company if I wanted to stoop to the methods some of the other guys use to get orders."

Neither regressions, nor rationalizations, nor any of the

many other "defense mechanisms" that psychologists have identified do in fact protect the self from itself. They are, at best, narcotics like drink or drugs. They serve merely to soften—and perhaps even that only temporarily—our feelings of failure. The danger lies not so much in their failure to protect us as in the fact that they discourage our efforts to improve ourselves. They deprive us of the opportunity of learning from our mistakes and reaching our true potential.

The morning session ends on this theme.

In the afternoon, the group leader asks the members if they have any problems with their superiors. There is no shortage of replies, many of them sharp: The boss is "too dominating," "too demanding," "not communicating clearly," "indecisive." He "fails to give credit for good work," "takes all the credit himself," "passes the buck," or "quickly passes the blame."

Then the group leader asks if the participants have any problems with those who are on the same level as they are.

There are plenty of answers to this question, too: people are not cooperative; they hunt for personal advantage; they are slow in making decisions, so as to let others make the mistakes; they play politics; and they butter up the boss.

"Finally," asks the group leader, "do you have any troubles with your subordinates?" The responses include the following: subordinates refuse to accept responsibility, avoid difficult jobs, never take risks, fail to communicate, lack a real desire to support the organization, and are exclusively concerned with their paychecks.

Having collected these problems with the higher-ups, the equals, and the lower-downs, the group leader then asks, "Did any of you happen to notice that whether you were talking about your bosses, your equals, or your subordinates, the problem was always the other person; the failing was always his, not yours? You didn't fail to win his confidence; he simply didn't give it. You didn't fail to get his support; he just withheld it from you.

"Does it occur to you now that some of you were projecting, rationalizing, defending yourselves? Is it possible that you were covering up your own shortcomings, your own inadequacies?

"I don't want you to think you're alone in this. If other T-groups can be used as a guide—and I feel they can—then you are still refusing to recognize your behavior as defensive. I think we still have some self-analyzing to do before we see ourselves as others see us."

CHAPTER VII

THE END OF ROUND ONE •

FRIDAY MORNING. It's 11:00 A.M., and the five T-groups have returned to the assembly hall where they first gathered five days before for their briefing session.

"Five days," Ken says. "It seems more like five years."

"Yes," says George, "light-years. Last Monday we were strangers. Now I feel I almost know you better than I know my wife."

"I look in the mirror as I shave," Ken exclaims, "and I ask myself if this is the same person. I don't feel the same. I take the stubble off my face, and I ask, 'Didn't I used to know you?'"

Ken is joking; he feels good. But there's a serious under-current in what he says. And the fellow he's joking with knows how he feels because he feels the same way.

One of the group leaders has gone to the rostrum to announce that this session is going to be a kind of debriefing.

He hopes all the men have had a valuable experience, hopes they'll be able to put what they've learned into practice.

The main purpose of this first unit has been to increase your understanding of yourself, of the people around you, and of the effect you have on them.

Most of this training you received in your T-groups. There each of you acted and reacted according to your own set of ideas about the kind of person you are and about how you function best.

As you proceeded, you've become aware of the way ideas and the feelings that accompany them are communicated. You've experimented. You've seen where the blocks to effective communication occur; you've examined the built-in filters created by your own emotions and inner needs. You've seen how these filters affect perception and reason, shape our ways of doing and knowing.

You've seen how they frustrate attempts to communicate with others whether in the sender or the receiver. A sender may be speaking but not really communicating. A receiver may be listening but not really hearing. You've learned, I hope, how to be a more effective sender, a better receiver.

I know you've taken away with you some understanding of the image of you you've aroused in others and how it compares with your own image of yourself. You may have come to recognize that there is wisdom in the old cliché that your best friend is also your severest critic. You discovered it was possible to build deep friendships whenever the benefits of criticism were recognized.

Most of what you've learned has come from critically examining the present—your behavior and the behavior of others toward you, here and now, in this training lab, this week.

Finally, underlying whatever you learned, whatever your

group leader and your group associates have tried to give you, has been a sincere hope that you would take it with you and use it when you got back home on the job.

We hope you've found it worthwhile. And when you come back for your second week, we'll be eager to hear about your experience in using those new insights and new skills in dealing with special problems you come up against in your own companies. Until then, good luck!

After hearing the parting speech, a trainee—who came to the T-group not because he felt he needed it but because his company sent him—commented, "If I'd heard anything like that a week ago, I'd have been—to put it mildly— highly skeptical. But I'll say this. I've talked more freely and been closer to the men here than I have with people in my company I've known for 25 years. For that alone this week at the lab has been worthwhile."

The four remarks which follow are typical of what others are saying:

What did I get out of it? I think if I started talking about this experience right now, I'd never stop. I just want to go home and see what happens with my job. But I'll say this: I feel good about it. I feel confident in a very comfortable way—keener, yet more relaxed. It's a good feeling.

I found it a real thrill. I mean just that. I got a kick even out of learning my faults. Not that I ever thought I was perfect. But to admit your faults to yourself, to be aware of them, and say what the hell, nobody's perfect—or to change if you can—that's something. The thing is to make the most of what you have, your own capabilities. And the only way to do that is to study yourself, to know what your potential is and understand how to reach it.

I'll add one thing to that. Along with finding out what we lacked, I think some of us discovered aspects of ourselves we never were fully aware of. A fellow may be afraid to look for something—afraid he might find it isn't there, that he doesn't really have it.

I have a lot to think about; I've learned, I've seen, I've observed. And I've understood more about myself. It's almost as though a kind of a weight has been lifted from my shoulders. I think I've learned not only how to deal with my business associates without causing resentment but even how to talk more honestly with all those about me.

CHAPTER VIII

THE SECOND WEEK: EMPHASIS ON THE GROUP •

V ERY OFTEN, WHEN a laboratory training program is laid out for three weeks, the three units are separated by a considerable interval of time. Between sessions the trainees have an opportunity to apply what they have learned, and at subsequent sessions they are expected to tell what happened and what new problems they have had to face.

The participants having concerned themselves primarily with interpersonal relations during their first week, the sessions in the second and third weeks emphasize intergroup relations, leadership roles, and the application of these to problems back on the job. The men experiment with new approaches to managerial problems, practice new ways of communication, examine new methods of motivation, and learn new techniques of participation.

These highly complex problems are analyzed in a realistic

work atmosphere. Participants learn how to become more skillful leaders or more responsible members of a group. They attend problem-analysis and problem-solving sessions in which they acquire the skills and the sensitivities needed to build more effective work groups.

At the opening session on Monday morning of the second week we find about 50 participants assembled in the hall. The composition of the groups changes for the second week, and the trainees find themselves working with men they didn't know before.

Very often, "planner" teams of three men each are formed and assigned the task of formulating proposals for the week's program. After each of the five teams has decided on a plan, the planners present it orally to all the members in a general session. One team may suggest setting up a holding company to acquire new enterprises. Another may propose organizing a management consulting firm. Still another may want to go back to the same unstructured approach used during the first week of the training lab.

The planner teams then try to recruit members by selling the superior merits of the plan they have outlined. Each participant is free in turn to join the group which suits him best. The give-and-take discussions between planners trying to persuade recruits and recruits reacting both to the proposals and the manner of persuasion provide the content for the T-group discussions with which the lab starts its inquiries.

For instance, they may discuss how the prospective team members responded to the overeager, "hard sell" manner of one of the planners. Why did another seem so unwilling to defend his committee's proposal, and how did his fellow team members react to his reluctance? Why was it that only two men in the whole assembly hall chose team *A*'s plan?

The discussion is focused on the behavior of each of the members, and the feedback flows. Comments are varied: "tried too hard," "too long-winded," "didn't seem wholehearted in his effort," "too dominating," "too submissive to authority," "too stuffy," "too highly organized," or "too disorganized."

PERFORMING UNDER STRESS

One of the first exercises during the second week aims to help group members see their weakness in coming to grips with the collective task of problem analysis and problem solving. On Tuesday morning the T-group is divided into two five-man committees: one to act as observers and give their comments; the other to make a relatively simple managerial choice such as whether to add more people to an already overloaded department or put the present staff on overtime.

What happens in the latter group forms a basis for discussion and analysis by the observers, but only after the members of this group themselves have analyzed—in front of the observers—their own strengths and weaknesses in reaching their decision. One of the men in the second group may be asked to lead the meeting so that the others can observe and comment on his conference-leadership style.

Then the roles are reversed, and the observers become members of the second committee. In this way both groups become sensitized to the forces at work in problem solving. The new observers are especially sensitive to the active but unexpressed jockeying for advantages that they discerned when they were outside looking in.

Sometimes a tape of the session is recorded and played back—often to the amazement of the committee members. This gives the behavior a different meaning: one member tries to impress the others; another seems afraid to disagree; a third argues over every issue; one man tries to dominate; another seems aloof; and, finally, the leader himself shows a lack of tact in dealing with a recalcitrant member. How each person affects all the others and their reactions to him is freely expressed.

The discussion opens up now, and both the observers and the members of the second committee dig deep into motives, feelings, and reactions. One member of the T-group may cite the "hidden agenda"—rivalry and antagonism between two members or the personal stake one man may have had in seeing the decision come out his way. Still another may assert that the reasons given for reaching the decision seem to have little connection with the underlying personal reasons revealed during the discussion. Or a man may observe that the decision was made by mere majority instead of with a general consensus.

At times, each member may be asked to rate his behavior on a series of items such as his tendency to be silent, to wander off the subject, to disagree, to assume leadership, to offer constructive ideas, and the like. The other members are then asked to rate each of the rest on the same items. The two ratings are compared, and the differences between the self-appraisal and the way others see the same behavior become part of the learning process.

Thus does the training lab combine an understanding of the process of group problem solving and the opportunity to experiment with new patterns of behavior—and receive immediate reaction and evaluation. In the T-group feedback, the men examine their reaction to the reluctance of some members to express their true feelings and the fear of others to dissent from majority opinion; the effect of yes men in the group and the influence of a too-strong leader; the role of the silent member and the general atmosphere of openness in the meeting. Throughout the discussion, the process of feedback continues as the men probe attitudes and behavior for the clues that will enable them to learn from their experiences.

T-group members experience varying degrees of anxiety as they try out new ways of building relationships with others. Those situations that arouse the strongest emotional reactions are likely to be similar to the ones they encounter in their own companies back home. Generally involved is conflict with fellow members whom they perceive as a threat to themselves. This gives rise to the greatest anxiety and the highest tension. It has been noted that frequently stress also grows out of the fear of being rejected by members of the groups or of not living up to the expectations of others, the fear of being hurt or disappointed, or the fear of being overruled.

Each lab participant tends to react to stress situations in ways that have proved satisfactory in the past. Now the task is to see how appropriate this behavior is in the here and now.

For instance, Ken says, "I didn't like John the first time we met several days ago. I find that I dislike him even more now. But last night I couldn't sleep and kept wondering about why I dislike him. He is pleasant to me, dresses nicely, gets along well with others. Suddenly it hit me. I don't like him because he has many of the traits I have and which I dislike in myself. He talks too much, puts on an intellectual air, pretends to be a good listener but is bored unless he is speaking, and always quotes authorities to back up his point of view. In addition, he has a tendency to interrupt others when they are speaking.

"Now I know, or at least I have become much more keenly aware in the last few days, how many of these same negative qualities I possess. I've made several decisions, therefore. I am going to try to listen a little more patiently and keep my mouth shut a great deal more. I'm making a pledge not to quote any outside authority for the rest of this week, and I'm not going to interrupt anyone else while he is speaking. Maybe John ought to try doing the same."

The task of meeting stress without such customary ego-supporting props as the title a man holds in the company and the assistants who always support him increases the anxiety and feelings of frustration the lab participant experiences. Reactions that might work in a man's own company meeting are ineffective in the free and frank atmosphere of the T-group. The fact that there is no pulling rank in a T-group and that a man has never been so much on his own is something every lab participant learns in sensitivity training.

In the T-group, therefore, some situations that the training leader sets up are aimed not at alleviating anxiety but at deliberately increasing the level of tension until each member's defense structure comes into play. Only when the anxieties aroused become too great and too threatening to some members will the T-group leader intervene.

Since few people see their behavior under stress clearly enough to perceive its real effect on others, feedback from the T-group, particularly during an exercise designed to provoke the men into revealing the way they react to anxiety, is immensely valuable, for it enables a lab participant both to measure the impact of his characteristic behavior in times of stress and to test out new and more effective responses.

ADDING THE ELEMENT OF COMPETITION

A second laboratory experiment in learning how to work together is made more complex by adding a competitive element. Each group sets out to prove its superiority over the other groups by competing in writing a two-page essay in one hour on the subject of "Money as a Factor in Motivation." One judge is selected from each of the competing groups. The judges are to decide which group paper can be rated as the best. The interest aroused in the competition is often intense.

The excitement is heightened when each group's papers are exchanged for reading. Each group assigns a spokesman to present and defend the claims of its paper before a general session of all the members. After this, each of the trainees (excepting only the judges) fills out a questionnaire on which he rates the various essays, naming the one he judges to be best and giving his opinion about the judge's capacity to make an impartial decision.

Meanwhile, the judges deliberate in the presence of all the T-group members and feelings run high. The judges then render their decision. Questions develop: Were the judges partial to their own groups? How does being on a losing team affect a man's attitudes toward the others? Is there evidence of "scapegoating"? By whom? Which members were most responsible for the poor showing? Whose ideas were most valuable? How do the trainees feel about the members who took over? Did the prediction of the members come close to the judges' decision?

The effects of win-or-lose competition on people are dramatically exposed. Group members take the rivalry seriously, and the anxiety and tension level rises. This brings out many kinds of personal behavior that are discussed by the members as soon as they return to their T-groups.

When the T-group settles down, John opens the discussion with a broadside attack on Lou. "Lou, you were our first choice for judge because we thought you would be fair and objective. But you were neither. You were so anxious to please the other judges that you bent over backward—you never presented the strong points of our essay at all."

Lou replies, "You are impossible to please. One day you accuse me of silence—and another time that I talk too much. Now I bend backward. Why are you always attacking me? Is it because you don't like people who are fair?"

Ralph enters with a defense of John: "I wasn't aware of any antagonism on John's part. I think his comments were fully justified. You seem to me to be the kind of person that has to control every situation, and you use a variety of tactics to maintain that control. If it suits your purpose, you can be agreeable and charming. If it doesn't, you can be so demanding that you are a pain in the neck."

Pete enters the discussion: "Another thing, Lou, that I seem to feel about you is that you never give a straight answer. There's always an evasion of some kind. Sometimes it's open; more often it's hidden. I wonder if you really do it consciously."

Lou breaks in with, "You fellows are always blaming someone for your own shortcomings. You push people around as if you didn't think they could fight back. Well I can; and if you feel I am disruptive and a loner, well, that's O.K. with me. I don't mind criticism. I like it. It doesn't bother me. It's strange, though, that I don't seem to antagonize people anywhere else except here."

John answers for the others: "I suspect you don't know when you antagonize people any more than the rest of us do. No one tells you. Well, what you do with other people I don't know. But I know that I find you constantly antagonistic. I admit you hide your manipulation of people behind a very smooth and amiable front—what someone has called the mask of manners. But you are pretty good at putting people on the defensive, even when you know you're wrong."

Lou interrupts again: "I say I'm fair and open-minded, and I don't think you like it. Do you want to win so badly that you would like to find me dishonest?"

John cuts in: "That last statement is exactly what I am talking about. You phrase every comment in such a way that a person can't answer it without conceding he's wrong or saying you're right.

"You did the same thing in the role playing. You constantly interrupted the other role players with such comments as, 'What are you trying to do—ruin this company?' Or, 'What do you think our company policy is? To deliver the goods late?' You talk about being warm and friendly and boast about belonging to more than 20 charitable organizations. But what comes out, to me at least, is a rock-crusher personality that has to dominate and control. Deep down I get the feeling you don't really like people."

Lou says: "John, why don't you fellows try taking me as I am? I have a feeling it's you who need to be changed, not me. Frankly I'm pretty well satisfied with the way I am."

Pete answers: "Lou, you don't have to justify yourself to anyone. I don't think any of us give a damn whether you like yourself the way you are or not. We're just trying to be helpful in letting you know how others see you. I can't crawl inside of you and make you see how sincere we are—it's your problem after we tell you what we see and feel about you."

The group leader then shifts the give and take to an appraisal of the way the representative of each T-group presented his essay to the judges.

Generally, T-group sessions begin with light banter and good-natured small talk. But being losers hurts most of the group members, and they often react with considerable anger. This makes it especially valuable for the learning process because it is possible for the group leader to point out the kinds of similar situations that can occur in a company when department heads are put into winner-loser situations.

For example, a number of department heads in a company may be seeking an increase in budget. Each tries to win approval for his demands irrespective of the merits of those of other departments. The decision may be reached by a slender majority vote. The losers have to abide by the decision, but inwardly they may feel a deep resentment that will create friction in other ways.

Members of the T-group learn that "victory" and "defeat" bring emotional reactions that can be detrimental to the company and harmful to their associates. They are encouraged to make a fresh examination of their own feelings and to explore alternatives to winner-loser situations.

THE EFFECT OF THE GROUP ON THE INDIVIDUAL

A third experiment is a variation of one developed by Robert R. Blake and Jane S. Mouton for use in their Managerial Grid Program. Its purpose is to demonstrate the influence of group membership on the individual. The 50 members again are assembled in the hall and given a written multiple-choice test on a series of managerial problems. They have 60 minutes to complete the test and return to their T-group rooms.

Then the same test is given again, but the answer to each of the questions must this time represent a consensus of each T-group. Two hours are allowed for each group to come up with its collective answers, but obviously this is not enough time for ten men to reach agreement on a large number of complex problems. As a result, considerable tension builds up as time runs out.

Finally the two types of answers are compared. The comparison sometimes shows that an individual scores higher working alone than the group scores working together. This indicates that he disregarded his own judgment under pressure from other members. This later becomes the subject for discussions: Why did the member who answered the questions most correctly in private fail to assert himself? Why did the other group members refuse to listen? How does the member learn to remain firm about the rightness of his position? When does he accept the joint judgment of his associates?

This exercise resembles meetings where the "best" solution for the company is passed over because of the dominating behavior of a forceful minority which imposes its position on some of the weaker members. Let's assume, for example, that a company controller is right in his belief that the company could operate with a smaller inventory. The sales manager may want a larger inventory so that from his departmental point of view he could offer improved customer service. The managers of warehousing, data processing, production, marketing, and insurance may go along with a decision that they privately disagree with rather than argue with a long-winded and stubborn associate. Such a solution is one that avoids conflict rather than one that seeks what is best for the company. This situation is typical of many company meetings where people with different points of view must work as a team.

In a T-group exercise, each member is put in the position of examining the process of reaching a decision and is alerted to the leadership skills needed. He is shown how interpersonal hostility and jockeying for power can be brought into the open. The feedback after this multiple-choice-test exercise is often heated and acrimonious.

The members of a T-group whose individual scores were

higher than the group score are obviously angry with each other.

George starts at once. "We sure turned out to be the dumbest group."

Sam shoots right back, "We had enough knowledge, but we allowed you to control the answers. That's where we were dumb."

"What do you mean?" George retorts. "I have only one vote, same as anyone else. On what do you base your statement that I controlled the answers?"

Larry breaks in to say, "I think Sam is right. The low score was a direct result of your high-pressure way of dominating our meeting. You're sharp and fast. You sound hostile when we disagree with you. You argue over the smallest detail until we give in because we feel like saying the hell with it. It doesn't mean we agree with you."

George cuts in fast. "Just wait a minute. No one had to vote for my answers. If you fellows have so little self-confidence and concede your answer is wrong even when you think it's right, why blame me? It's your own weakness, not mine. You say yes when you mean no, and you blame me."

The atmosphere becomes tense. It is probably clear to the group leader that a highly emotional conflict is about to break into the open. But he refrains from stepping in.

Phil interrupts. "George, that last comment is typical of your attitude toward all of us. You're sharp and you know it. But here's something you *don't* know: you don't know why you need to have your own way all the time, why you argue over every trifle. The rest of us don't act that way. We feel the group is too important to waste our time arguing about insignificant items. Personally I feel that we've put up with your attitude long enough."

"I'm tired of you people leaning on me," George replies. "Everyone has an equal chance to be heard and to influence the rest; and if you are that easily persuaded, heaven help your companies. I'd hate to have a bunch of rubber stamps like you working for me!"

Sam re-enters the discussion. "I wonder if you really know the kind of yes men you must have on your staff. You have a blind spot on this subject that keeps you from seeing how obnoxious your manner is. I'm not talking about your ability; you've got plenty. And you're an able speaker, the most articulate member of the group. But you don't seem to realize how you bulldoze everyone else by your manner. I think you'd be a great success in a one-man company. But in a big outfit the only men who would work with you and not resign would be the weak ones—those who were willing to let somebody else do all the thinking."

George answers with impatience: "Do you think you've said anything constructive—all you want to do is to find a scapegoat."

But Sam is not ready to give up. Instead, he continues, "George, you're a terrific fellow in many ways, but I think you are a handicap to this group; and from what you've just said, I really think we're not the best group for you. We're not helping you much. I'm going to propose that we ask you to leave. Maybe you'll fit better elsewhere. I'm convinced we'll get nowhere this week with you here."

A couple of minutes later the group votes to ask George to leave them and to see if he can be accepted in one of the other groups.

This reaction does not occur often. But it does happen—just as on some rare occasion when a member will tell the others he feels he could work more effectively in another T-group. Usually, after an incident of this kind, the conference leader will spend some time alone with the man in question. Then, very often, the man returns to the group—but now keenly aware of his impact on the other members.

CHAPTER IX

BARRIERS TO COMMUNICATION •

THE THEORY SESSION on Wednesday morning of the second week is often focused on barriers to communication. In this particular case, an executive named Henry, who has had 20 years' experience in radio and television, is asked to meet with two other executives to prepare a report on "Ways of Failing and Succeeding in Communication."

Henry begins that report as follows:

I have jotted down a number of aphorisms which are expressive of what seems to be a national disposition to discourage person-to-person communication—and this in a land where communication as a technology and way of life has reached its apogee. Here are a few of them:

- Silence is golden.
- No news is good news.
- Better to be silent and be thought a fool than to speak and remove all doubt.

- Children should be seen and not heard.
- What you don't know won't hurt you.
- Anything you say may be held against you.
- Talk is cheap.

I would like to apologize for the brief report. My excuse sounds contrived, but there really was a "failure of communication" with the other two members. We were all talking, but nobody was listening. Each of us had a different idea of when and where we were supposed to get together. Anyway, even if we had met, I doubt that we could have found many phrases that encouraged rather than suppressed communication.

After he finishes reading, Henry suggests that what he read could well be an indication of a reluctance on the part of American adults to enter into warm and open relationships with one another. "I think this is unfortunate," he says. "It would be useful to learn whether people really know the things about ourselves that we assume they don't know. It would be valuable, too, to have others tell us things about ourselves that we don't know."

To which Ed observes, "Your excuse sounds as convincing as a TV commercial. I hope, though, that you mean it about wanting to discover what others feel about you. The fact is you impress me as a kind of cold, noncommunicative customer yourself. I've been trying to figure out why. I think part of it is the sort of words you use, which are cold and logical words like 'technology,' 'aphorism,' and 'apogee.' It's also partly your tone of voice. It's full of self-control. When you say 'Good morning,' you make it sound like 'Stay out of my way if you know what's good for you.' I haven't heard you say anything friendly or pleasant since you got here. Nor unhappy, either. If you have warm feelings, where do you hide them?"

Henry replies, "I don't happen to be the emotional type.

Oh, I can lose my temper, but what's the point? Where does it get you? It certainly doesn't help you get along in *my* business."

"I'm not talking about temper," Ed tells him. "I'm talking about your opening up. I sometimes wonder what you feel behind that poker face. No one here knows who you really are. We're all here to learn something about ourselves. Most of us have discussed things we wouldn't ordinarily talk about. But not you. You repress all your emotions. We came here to help one another. How can anyone help *you*? We can't even get to know you. Looking at you this very moment, I don't know how you feel about what I'm saying. There seems to be no response at all. Are you hurt or indifferent or pleased? I can't tell."

Henry replies slowly. "What's unusual about holding back your feelings? Don't we all? Look, you say to somebody, 'How are you?' Do you really expect a truthful answer? You don't. Why? Because we don't go around telling everybody how we feel."

Here Pete joins in. "Henry, you're evading the real issue. The real issue is you. I feel about you as Ed does. I think you imagine that if you reveal a confidence, you will destroy your relationship with others, that later you may be sorry you said it or that people may think less of you. I guess this is how we all feel sometimes. But you seem to feel this way all the time. You keep your feelings under a lid. When are you going to open up?"

"You're kidding yourself," Henry answers. "Why should any of us really uncover our hidden feelings? Who can we talk to about our deeply personal problems? Who really wants to hear about my problems or yours? Who really cares? Nobody.

"There's enough pain in this world. Why should I, for example, inflict my hurt on you? How will that help either of us? How is it going to improve our relationships if I spill my guts to you?"

Henry's question is picked up quickly by Frank. "You know what I think, Henry? I think you're a lonely guy and easily hurt, and I'd bet it isn't doing you any good in your job. You got where you are by being bright but aloof, by watching out for every chance and playing it cool. But you could get set back that way, too. You could be eased out of a top position—if there's a change in your company's power structure, for instance—just because you are such an ice cube. Maybe they don't dislike you. But they might just have the feeling you don't like them. How can you build relationships of mutual trust and liking when you don't give of yourself?"

Frank continues, "And what's the reason? Well, I'm no psychiatrist, not even an amateur one, but here you are, a guy with feelings—though you hate to admit it—and the chances are you've been hurt, maybe early in your life. As I say, I don't know, but I'd bet on this. When you say you don't want to cause pain or inflict your troubles on other people, isn't it because you don't expect them to give a damn and you think it will only make things worse for you?"

Seymour picks up the discussion. "That's just how it looks to me, Henry. I think maybe it's because you're scared. There's probably a fancier word for it, but I say you're afraid—afraid that people will think less of you. But you're wrong about that. We all have the same doubts inside; but we let go, we laugh, we get happy, we get angry, we feel. You seem to think you've got to swallow your anger, your hurts, your feelings. And that stuff is poisonous. It's better to let it out of your system—better for you, better for your company."

"Thanks, Seymour," Henry replies. "I'll make a note of

your suggestion." He pauses for emphasis and then adds, "And file it." But he doesn't sound as breezy and confident as he obviously is trying to sound. He is aware that the group has reached him at a deeper level than he can admit, and his real feelings have come too close to the surface for him to express them with comfort.

Sal takes it from there. "I go along with Seymour. If we can get behind that front of yours, Henry, and get you to put out a bit of honest emotion, I'll feel we've accomplished something. If I had an employee or a business colleague like you, I'd try my damnedest to get through to him. And if I didn't, after a long, hard try, I think we'd have to part company. He'd make me too uncomfortable."

Henry asks, "Do I make you uncomfortable?"

"You do, yes."

"How? What do I do?"

"It isn't what you do, it's what you *don't* do. That's what we're trying to tell you. I'm going to ask a question." Sal turns to the group seated at the table. "Will those who feel as I do about Henry, here, raise their hands?"

When Henry sees seven hands go up, he stops looking chipper and for a moment loses his breezy air. He really looks thoughtful.

Change does not come easily to people like Henry. A few observations will not make some member suddenly change lifelong habits. Many long hours and, at times, many days are needed to get through to somebody like Henry. Sometimes the mask never comes off, and the man remains defensive. No one can get through to him.

Members vary in their response to personal feedback. Some solicit it; others avoid it, though they really want this probing, this assistance. After all, it's one of the reasons they're in the T-group. And there are very few men who go through such an experience without feeling in the end that it has been valuable. Usually they admit it before they go home at the end of the first week. Occasionally they don't. But by the end of the third week few trainees deny it.

Henry does respond during the coffee break. He grins at Seymour and says, "You're getting under my thick hide. It was that show of hands. Seven! That's something to think about. Damn if it isn't."

After the coffee break, the group leader suggests they try an interesting exercise. He notices that two members, Bill and Ed, have not yet returned. He proposes to the others an experiment that will demonstrate the effect of group action on the behavior of the individual.

He suggests that for the rest of the meeting that afternoon they ignore any comment or suggestion that comes from Bill. With Ed, they will do just the opposite. They will pay profuse attention to him. "Well," he says, "here they come. Let's see what happens."

Several minutes later, Ed speaks up. The group listens attentively and comments favorably. Whereupon he has another idea to offer, and another, and another. All his ideas receive the same treatment. The number and swiftness of Ed's contributions seem to be in direct proportion to the appreciation they get. Before long, Ed is participating more freely than he has all week. His ideas are making sense, too. Many of them would have deserved and would have received unplanned attention.

On the other hand, being ignored, Bill lapses into complete silence. At first, as his observations are rejected or ignored, it seems to annoy him. For a while he tries even harder and increases his efforts to get attention. Failing in this, he belittles the others for not seeing his point. Still ignored, he becomes uncertain; he risks fewer and fewer observations. Finally he falls silent and keeps himself out of the discussion.

Near the close of the session, the leader reveals to a startled Ed and Bill the nature of the experiment that has been carried on without their knowledge. He points out to the entire group how its attitudes have influenced the self-image and subsequent behavior of Bill and Ed. The leader then tells the group about a classic experiment designed by the social psychologist Solomon Asch to demonstrate the same effect on a more scientific basis.

Asch presented a series of identical cards to a number of groups of eight people. Each card was marked with lines of slightly different lengths. He had arranged in advance with seven members of each group that they would agree that all of the lines were identical in length. Thus there was one person in each group of eight who, even though he perceived the lines as differing in length, found himself a minority of one when the results were announced. Could he stand alone against the seven? Asch tried the experiment on about 100 groups. In over 60 per cent of them, the lone individual changed his judgment to conform to the judgment of the seven.

Seymour comments on this experiment by recalling that he had a boss once who criticized or ridiculed every idea he didn't like. He was so abusive toward anyone calling attention to something wrong that his department heads either made no comment or covered up mistakes and shifted the blame. The boss heard only optimistic reports. The only operating figures he was shown were juggled ones. High overhead was "a temporary difficulty," heavy production costs were "one-time, starting-up expenses," and dissatisfied customers were "chronic complainers." Finally the time came when things could no longer be hidden. The boss demanded to know why he wasn't told sooner. Who would dare to tell him why? Who could tell him why he never was told the truth?

Ralph interrupts to say, "He sounds like the president of my company at our weekly meetings. The president invites open discussion. He thinks he's open-minded, democratic—says he's proud of our free and open discussions. But just let somebody disagree with him, and he cuts the discussion short. He glares at us and says, 'We've discussed this long enough, haven't we?' " Ralph's description of his boss causes general laughter.

Then Ed wants to know how the group would manage a situation in which two capable department heads always argue with each other and never resolve any of their differences. He has in mind the production chief and sales manager of his own company. How can they be brought together?

The suggestion is made that an answer might be found in a procedure devised by Carl Rogers to stop the kind of endless argument between people that never comes to any clear conclusion. "Let's try this procedure ourselves," the group leader suggests. "We begin by agreeing that no one can state his own point of view without first restating what the other person has said. The restatement has to be acceptable to the person who first made it. Back-and-forth discussion cannot proceed until each speaker has correctly stated the position of his antagonist. Then he can state his own."

The T-group finds it very difficult to implement this procedure. Ken complains that it requires him to listen so hard to get what each speaker is saying that he can't concentrate on what he wants to say when his turn comes. Once or twice a speaker and his opponent have to repeat themselves three or four times before they can agree on what was said. But the group finds the process absorbing.

Seymour observes that under the Rogers rule the discussion is considerably calmer than all but the most casual conversation. Nobody breaks in on a speaker before he has completed his thought. Pete calls attention to the fact that the slowing-up process has brought a change of emphasis. Participants are no longer so concerned about winning the argument or proving themselves right. They want, instead, to achieve an understanding. And if arguments are not to be won, they can't be lost. Neither party suffers injury or loses face. Everyone is concerned about reaching agreement.

Henry observes that not only does the listener have to give close attention to what the speaker is saying, but the speaker himself becomes keenly aware of how what he is saying sounds to the others. Consequently, the speaker is more careful in choosing words that will convey his meaning. "I didn't mean it that way" becomes a recurrent theme during the experiment.

The total effect of the Rogers procedure is summed up in Sal's closing remark. "This is one idea I'm going to take home with me—and not just to the office."

CHAPTER X

WINDING UP THE WEEK •

On THURSDAY, THE DISCUSSION turns to the need for improved interviewing skills. This is a subject that concerns most lab participants because so much of every manager's day is spent in face-to-face communication. Here the men are introduced to the two main categories of interviewing: directive and nondirective. A good manager, they are told, will use either or both as the situation demands. The group leader then goes into a little explanation:

In most cases when we want information, we simply ask for it. If the interview is being conducted to gather factual data, the easiest method of getting this information is to ask the person who is supposed to have it.

But in many cases questioning that becomes too direct has limitations. The person interviewed will realize what the interviewer is seeking and will slant his answers to make himself appear in the most favorable light. When an interviewer is looking for information that is less apparent or less specific, an indirect method of interviewing may prove more fruitful.

Nondirective interviewing is based on the principle of taking a sounding-board approach to the interviewee and accepting emotions as they are presented. The interviewer makes no attempt to direct the course of the conversation. He turns his full attention to listening, attempting to discover not only words, but also feelings, attitudes, and emotions.

By fully accepting all the responses of the person interviewed without expressing criticism or judgment, the interviewer encourages these responses and gains information that could be obtained in no other way. The nondirective approach has an added advantage: it allows the person interviewed to arrive at self-insights, and these insights are thus more likely to be accepted.

A feature of the nondirective method is the avoidance of questions that lead to direct answers. Emphasis is on the present, rather than on the past. A permissive, accepting atmosphere is maintained throughout the interview.

The group leader then demonstrates interviewing by the nondirective method. He asks a member named Mort to take the part of the person being interviewed.

"I will play the interviewer," he says. "Let's assume you are a machinist, a good one. And you're intelligent and friendly. About a year ago you were promoted to foreman and great things were expected of you. However, your performance rating shows some limitations. Some of your men have been complaining that they would like more opportunity to talk with you, but that you are difficult to reach. Also, they feel that you could show more interest in them.

"We'll start the interview. You're in my office. I am the production manager."

INTERVIEWER: How are you, Mort? How is everything on the job?

MORT: Well, I feel it's going reasonably well.

INTERVIEWER: You mean it could be better in some ways?

MORT: Well, everything could be better. Well, I guess there are some difficulties with two men who have not shaped up as well as I had hoped. Part of it might be my fault.

INTERVIEWER: You have a feeling that you and the men aren't getting along well?

MORT: Yes. I wouldn't go so far as to say I'm sure, but it's a feeling I have.

INTERVIEWER: Do you think that being promoted to foreman has anything to do with it?

MORT: I suppose so. My job . . . you know, I've stepped up. I feel I have to be a little more formal, and the fellows I used to work with . . . I guess they resent it.

INTERVIEWER: You think that some of the men may feel that you haven't paid enough attention to them?

MORT: Well, I guess some of them could feel neglected because I haven't been around with them too much, and maybe they assumed I wasn't satisfied with them.

INTERVIEWER: Well, what do you think we can do to solve this problem and make them feel differently?

The group leader stops at this point. He says, "Notice, first, that the questions have been so put as to lead the foreman to state the problem of his men's feelings about him and that he is ready to do something about it. The questioning gradually brought to Mort a realistic understanding of the problem on which corrective measures could be based.

"Suppose now we break up into threes, each of the three taking his turn at being the interviewer, the interviewee, and the observer."

The leader then suggests several situations that could be used for practice sessions, and the members begin to evaluate and analyze one another's weaknesses in conducting the nondirective interview.

REVIEWING BACK-HOME APPLICATIONS

At last the time comes to review back-home applications of the first week's learnings. The group leader invites volunteers to report on failures as well as successes.

Bill speaks up. "I had a failure. I delegated responsibility for a certain task to two subordinates. They seemed eager enough to accept it. But I made a mistake. I checked up on them too often. They lost interest. They seemed to think I didn't really trust them to handle the matter. So they started coming to me for directions. I thought it was less trouble to finish the job myself."

"I can see where I failed," he continues. "I admit it, I'm a perfectionist. I'm always afraid somebody else may not do the job right. But now I've made up my mind that perfectionist or not I'm really going to delegate some authority and allow my subordinates to carry on—on their own."

On the other hand, Phil has a success to report. He undertook an improvement in communication, a simple thing but one he had never tried before. His salesmen and production men just weren't pulling together, and customer complaints about quality were seriously cutting into repeat sales.

Phil reports: "So I decided to make a complete change from the past. The way I used to handle it, I would go to the plant and have it out with the production manager. This time, I invited 20 salesmen and 20 production men, including the quality control foremen, to a two-day meeting. I arranged that the 40 should be gathered in four groups of ten each—five from sales, five from production. The agenda called for each individual salesman to spend up to ten minutes discussing with one quality foreman the customer complaints that had come to him. After ten minutes, the salesmen in each group swapped partners and presented their problems to a different foreman.

"As soon as the cycle within each section was completed, the sections were rotated. This was repeated until each salesman had met individually with each production man. The problems were theirs; so were the solutions. They cooperated because they got to understand each other's problems."

"I must say," Phil tells the T-group, "the results were excellent. I found that out ten days later when each foreman reported to the plant manager on the corrective action he had taken. Sixty-one out of 62 quality complaints were eliminated with practically no extra cost. During the next three months there were no recurring incidents of poor quality."

SUMMING IT UP

Friday comes more quickly than the men realize. Some members have been up most of the night continuing the process of analyzing behavior, probing attitudes, and evaluating performance: feedback continues until the last moment. Where just a day earlier some of the men were dejected and others upset, all are now in good spirits. Realities have been confronted, anxieties relieved, new understanding acquired.

At the general "debriefing" session, attended by all of the participants, one of the T-group leaders summarizes the aims and purposes of the second week:

We carried forward, during the week just completed, the process of introducing you to yourselves. We hope this has given you greater knowledge and greater awareness of your impact on others. If you are like other groups that have completed this second week of training, you have a better understanding of group dynamics and of group process, because your practice in conducting meetings has given you a deeper understanding of what it means to be both a useful member and an aggressive leader of a group session.

You have had an opportunity to examine the factors that encourage the people in a group to cooperate and work together. You have considered and evaluated the ground rules for getting things done and for creating an atmosphere in which conflicts can be resolved without breaking up the group.

The need to respect individual feelings and individual needs has been emphasized, particularly in dealing with questions affecting the exercise of authority, the rivalries among sub-groups, and the struggle for executive power. You have experienced and evaluated the techniques of group decision making and group problem solving. In studying group behavior, you have seen how communication can collapse, and you have learned that a soliloquy is not a good form of communication.

You have observed the infinite capacity that exists in all of us for self-deception. You have watched at first hand how illusions can be taken for reality and how our blind spots keep us from seeing what is obvious to others. You have learned how differently things can be perceived through the eye of different beholders.

You may have explored new ways not only to run a business or head a department but even to live a life. I hope you will experiment with them when you return home.

We haven't offered you any magic—no nerve tonics, no virility restorers. We have not pretended to be soothsayers nor passed ourselves off as mystics. Whatever you have learned has been through your own efforts. You took off your masks, faced the truth, and found your real selves. What you found is now the foundation on which you can build.

We believe strongly that no help can be either wise or enduring if it does not lead to self-help. You have spent the week helping yourselves. You have gone beyond "live and *let* live" to "live and *help* live."

You are familiar with the way you can use the principles and practices of behavior you've learned here in your companies back home. We consider the practice of management to be an art in the same way that the practice of medicine is an art. But there are scientific principles that must be used in the practice of both. Managing people is developing these principles today. Effective management now requires scientific knowledge of the principles of human behavior as they are applied in industrial organizations.

I hope you will carry out the spirit of the lab in your daily activities. Diagnose, interact, encourage feedback, and experiment. Then come back in a couple of months and tell us what happened.

CHAPTER XI

APPLYING WHAT HAS BEEN LEARNED •

THE LAST WEEK of a typical three-week training lab is at once the most structured, the most challenging, and the most directly related to on-the-job problems the lab participant is likely to face back home. It provides opportunities to test both the interpersonal skills acquired during the first week in the lab and the understanding of organizational and group dynamics developed in the second. And it helps the men prepare a self-development program they will be able to follow after they have left the T-group.

Unlike the beginning of the first week, when T-group members are given no assignments to carry out and no agenda to follow, the third week loses no time in confronting the trainees with three major problems in decision making. All involve the four main topics on the week's agenda: leadership, organizational effectiveness, motivation, and managing change.

First, each ten-man T-group is required to divide itself into two subgroups of five men—not arbitrarily but on the basis of common interests among the trainees, the participants' individual needs, and the subgroup's own requirements—and come up with solid reasons for its decision within two hours. This task challenges the men to study their colleagues closely, both in terms of their personalities (How will we get along together?) and in terms of their potential contribution to the group (Is Jack likely to make a real contribution to the group? Will Harold throw his weight around too much?).

T-groups are often unwilling to face up to the task and, for example, propose (not always facetiously) to put tall men in one group and short men in another. But this passes quickly when someone reminds the men that each T-group will have to justify why it divided into two groups as it did and that the inability to present a reasonable explanation will indicate a failure both to face reality and meet responsibility. Some groups are unable to probe deeply enough within the two-hour deadline: at one session, four men refused at the end of an hour and a half to discuss it any further, rose as one from the table, got another impatient member to join them, and formed a five-man group of their own. Most T-groups, however, seek to strike a balance between, say, aggressive and passive members, top and middle management representatives, and production men and sales executives in the formation of subgroups. Others seek to find common job interests, responsibilities, or difficulties with people as the basis for forming into the two groups—in anticipation of selecting the topic on which they will be spending most of their time during the week ahead.

Apparently, the simple task of dividing into two groups has so many back-home applications for the company executive—evaluating individuals, putting together a team, arriving at a group decision—that it serves as a stimulating beginning to what the T-group members find a deeply rewarding week.

Once the T-groups are formed into subgroups they face their next deadline: by the following morning they must select a leader and agree on a subject on which to concentrate during the remainder of the week.

The contest for leadership and maneuvering for the position of subgroup leader reveal a variety of behavior patterns that the training leader observes closely; later he joins with the group as a whole in analyzing the significance of each man's approach to the question.

Whether he comes right out and asks for the job or indicates by subtle means that he can serve the group best, the typical T-group member seeks the prestige, the power, and the satisfaction of leadership. Not infrequently, however, the men who aggressively pursue the job of leader are rejected by the subgroup in favor of someone who has demonstrated leadership qualities in the first assignment— splitting into two five-man sections.

The process reveals the men who are afraid of being rejected as group leaders or who inwardly doubt their ability to exercise leadership. One comments, "After all, this is only a practice session, and it doesn't really matter whether you're chosen as a leader or not." Another rationalization is frequently put in these terms: "I exercise enough leadership back home. Here in the lab I want to get practice in being a follower. Let someone else take over." More frequently, however, the man who at first declines the suggestion that he assume the subgroup's leadership is only waiting for more support; he has usually managed by this time to get across his qualifications for the job.

Some groups pick their chairman first and then decide

what topic to cover during the week. Others do it in reverse order, selecting their leader after they've gone through the process of choosing an area of study. The process of choosing one of the four listed topics for its program for the week—leadership, self-evaluation, instruction, and change —the subgroup must agree on a subject that all five members are concerned with and resist the member who urges as the topic for the group the problem that concerns him most.

The most important thing, however, is not what subject or which leader is selected but what process is adopted for carrying the selection out. The men are particularly sensitive to the process because they know that part of the assignment is to present their choices—of group, leader, and topic—to the general meeting of all the T-groups on Tuesday morning; and each group wants to come out looking best.

There are significant variations in these presentations, providing more material for analysis and evaluation by the men and their training leaders later during the week. Some subgroups present their account of how decisions were reached by means of their leader, who carries full responsibility for describing the process by which the subgroup was formed, a leader elected, and a topic chosen. Other subgroups share the responsibility for making the presentation among two or three of their members. Frequently, a subgroup will assign one member to serve as secretary and record its deliberations for use in the Tuesday-morning presentation. Here again it is the process of group development and leadership functioning, rather than the content of the discussions and decisions, that provides a meaningful experience for the T-group members.

Shortly after these presentations are made, the subgroups go off on their own, without a training leader, spending the rest of the day on their self-assigned projects. By Wednesday morning, the men in each subgroup have become deeply involved in their project and in each other. There is a feeling of mutual helpfulness and mutual trust; a team spirit has developed. Suddenly, without prior notice, the men are notified that the elected leader of each of the subgroups is to be transferred to a different subgroup.

It is a situation that occurs often enough in industry, when a manager will be moved from one department, one branch, or one city to another and the men he's been working with must adjust to a new boss as he must adjust to a new employee group. In the training lab, the sudden switch in subgroup leaders comes as a shock and provides a significant test of how both leader and group function under stress.

For the man who is transferred, the problem is to give up his personal association and psychological investment in his original subgroup and his chosen topic, to adjust quickly to his new team, to develop an interest in their problem, to show he understands it, and to win the respect and confidence he must have if he is to function effectively as a leader.

For the four remaining members of each subgroup, the tasks are equally difficult. Although their new leader is one they neither knew nor chose, they must forget about their old chief and bring the new man on board quickly, despite the resentment they may feel toward him. Occasionally such hostility becomes overt, and the men make no bones about their lack of enthusiasm for their new leader. In turn, his reaction may be equally strong as he tries to show who's boss by dominating the "company" meeting at which the plans for covering the subgroup's topic are whipped into shape.

This process also offers valuable lessons to the T-group

participants. For the new leader, there is the anxiety of being separated from his people, the task of establishing rapport with men likely to resent his very presence, the frustration of having to start all over again. But there is also the opportunity to experiment with different styles of leadership and to compare results from one subgroup to the other. For the group members confronted with the loss of their old leader, there is separation anxiety and feelings of abandonment. The requirement of adjusting to a new, strange leader creates the possibility of a power contest to fill the vacuum created by the departure of the original man. But there is also the challenge of pitching in harder until he is able to take over.

But the shock of the switch in leaders is mild compared to that of their next task. Again without prior notice, each subgroup is told on Thursday morning that it must choose one member of its five to be dropped from the team: He is to be the man whose contribution has been least valuable to the group, the man whom the others can best get along without.

Every company has this problem; almost every president or other top official who carries this responsibility keeps putting the job off. Procrastination then becomes the thief of profits as well as time—all the more reason why an executive with a sense of responsibility should not hesitate to act. The emotional strain on the executive who knows he ought to let an inefficient man go but who can't face up to it and keeps getting frustrated at the man's continued failure is still another price that must be paid.

In meeting this simulated situation in the laboratory, the T-group members must apply all the sensitivity and skill they have acquired during their training experiences. It is often difficult to tell who finds the experience more harmful: the man who is rejected by his teammates or the other four in each group who agree that he must go. Sometimes a member may say, "You can get along better without me. I'll be the goat and leave the group." But this may not be accepted by the others. The member to be dropped must defend himself; no one is permitted to resign. The least useful member of the group must leave, but only after he has made every effort to stay.

There are many reasons for dropping a member. Frequently, the man to be dropped will be the quiet, withdrawn member who has participated least or who hasn't given his teammates the opportunity to know him. Or he may be one of the most active members of the subgroup, the one who may have played a strong role but is rejected for a very patronizing manner which causes resentment among his fellow group members.

In one subgroup a man who spent the better part of two days helping his teammates carry out the topic which he had had a part in choosing—an intricate and detailed study of group influence and individual leadership—was asked to leave the group for this reason: "We think you've done wonders for us; we know we couldn't have accomplished it ourselves. But as smart as you are, we don't trust you. We have the feeling that you are a manipulator. If someone's got to go, you're the one."

Occasionally, the new chairman, transferred to the group the day before, is the one to be eliminated because—unlike the group's original leader—he has proved unable to gain the confidence of the subgroup.

All of the men who have been dropped by their groups now meet to compare what it's like to be eliminated and, more important, to explore among themselves the reasons why. In this session they are helped by "counselors" assigned to talk frankly with them and to help them acquire insight into the reactions and feelings of the members who rejected them and to suggest how they can learn from this experience in their back-home situation. There is a next time at the lab too: each man rejected by his subgroup is assigned to one of the other subgroups. Here he has the opportunity to function as a group member again and to experiment with new ways of becoming valuable to the group in attaining its goals.

On a rare occasion a member who has been dropped refuses to recognize the group's evaluation of his behavior. One man rejected by his subgroup during a lab session wouldn't budge from his original expression of resentment and rationalization—after 11 solid hours with his counseling team. This was a rare occurrence: there was general agreement that the man needed professional counseling. Most of the time the eagerness of the groups to help the men they've dropped gets through.

Assigning their former teammates to new groups is the responsibility of the subgroups themselves. The purpose is to put them in groups where they'll receive the most help and develop most quickly during the time that remains. This requires a close understanding of not only the weaknesses and strengths of the men who have been dropped but also the composition, leadership, and topic of the new group they are going to. The men carry this out with a degree of competence and a feeling of responsibility few would have thought themselves capable of before going into laboratory training.

The final phase of the exercise requires the four men who remain to welcome the new member that has been assigned to them and to integrate him into their own group activity. Part of the integration process includes further counseling of the new man: not just to brief him on the goals of his new team but to help him understand the behavior that caused him to be dropped and to improve his self-knowledge so that he will become more aware of the impact he makes on others.

The simulated dismissal exercise provides the kind of laboratory experience that requires the trainee to examine his own relative contributions to the group and also to measure—publicly and openly—the contributions of others, all in an atmosphere that must take into account the feelings of both the person rejected and the men who do the rejecting.

T-group members generally find this final week in the lab not only the most intensive but the most helpful in a practical way. The team project in the laboratory offers a veritable microcosm of the problems the executive is likely to face back home. Equally important, it provides an opportunity to measure his personal effectiveness—and be rated by his colleagues—as profound as any he is likely to encounter in his lifetime.

The subgroups continue in session until noon on Friday. Then all meet for a farewell lunch. The atmosphere is friendly and lively. All the members intermingle—no more T-groups. The seating at the tables is informal. Wives are invited to attend, and certificates and sometimes a group photograph are presented to all participants following the lunch. A short talk bidding all farewell is delivered by one of the conference leaders or, on special occasions, by an invited guest. But the atmosphere remains informal; and as soon as the brief ceremony is over, the members quickly pack and leave for home.

Some members take the opportunity to stay on so that they can spend a little extra time talking with a conference leader. Occasionally a participant will describe the way his attitude and behavior have changed in the three weeks he has spent in the lab:

I began to feel a little apprehensive about going into the lab before the first week began. I had heard the sessions are likely to get pretty rough. I wondered whether I was going to like the idea of putting myself under the microscope. I told myself: "I know I have faults, but why should they be brought out into the open?" I thought about dreaming up some "urgent" company business that would get me out of the deal; but after thinking it over for a day or so, I decided not to chicken out. Who was I kidding, anyway?

That first day of the first week, though, I decided to play it cool, just watch and see what happened. Let the big talkers take over. Most of Monday I kept my guard up, spoke up only when I was called on or when it was my turn to introduce myself or to describe my company.

The next day my idea of keeping my eyes open and my mouth shut seemed to be working fine. Why did I need people to tell me what they thought of me? Why should I tell anyone else what I knew about myself? The only thing that bugged me was that maybe they knew things about me that I didn't suspect. Or did they? It might help to find out what others see in the way I act, how they rate me as a person. Then I began to get nervous.

By Wednesday morning I was so tense about how the others saw me that I found myself looking for an opportunity to talk. Pretty soon someone threw a question at me about why I had been so silent, and I found myself saying things I had never told anyone before.

It's amazing how many things I had been building up inside me that I wanted to say and yet never opened up about. Before I knew it, I was talking a blue streak. Maybe it was because everyone seemed sympathetic, or at least interested. I felt safe because I had the feeling they were going to help me straighten out. At home and on the job I wouldn't think of admitting any weaknesses. Yet it is these very secret weaknesses that cause us to worry about losing our jobs or our promotions. If we could only talk these things out instead of keeping our fears to ourselves—if the people we work with could only develop enough confidence to "let go," we'd straighten out a lot of problems we never even dared to admit existed.

It took this kind of permissive atmosphere to bring my deepest feelings to the surface—and give me an idea of the kind of person I really am.

What happened was that the first things people told me about myself were negative, and the first things I told them about myself were always positive. Then as we got to know one another better, I began to recognize some of the negative things they found in me, and they began to find some positive qualities I didn't even know I possessed.

The second week got down to cases even faster. That's when I learned that unless I was willing to stick my neck out, I was going to have to give up any hopes of a leadership position in the T-group because I had nothing to offer. My teammates saw me as a guy who could be moved in either direction. Suddenly a lot of things that had happened to me back on the job fell into place. Just a couple of months before I had missed out on an important promotion. Now I know why.

But it was the third week that really got to me. The day I was dropped by my team as one of the least valuable members, I cried. It was that old bugaboo again—I didn't stand for anything. I hated those guys at first, but I've got to admit they had me down pat.

I'm going back home now. I know what I've got to work on—and work on it I will. I understand myself better. It was a salutary shock to hear the group verdict to oust me. I knew then they saw me for the person I was—but I pretended I was not.

I know I will have to wrestle with false fronts to find the true self deeply buried in my psyche. But I feel confident I now have the courage and the competence to know myself without distortion or partiality.

CHAPTER XII

BACK HOME •

As THE T-GROUP GRADUATES LEAVE for home, almost all
agree they have undergone a strenuous and stimulating
learning experience. However, in the minds of many there
are two questions:

1. How lasting will my new competence in managing
   people be back home?
2. Will the organizational structure of my company
   permit me to put this new knowledge to work?

The answers to these questions are important, for unless
the T-group member can turn his greater managerial competence into improved performance on the job, the experience will be frustrating to him and of little use to his
company. Yet neither question can be answered for weeks
—perhaps months—after the lab participant has returned

home. Moreover, the answer will depend a great deal on the company's policies and managerial practices. This is one reason so many participants say to their training leaders as they shake hands in farewell, "I hope I can get the boss to take lab training."

If the president of the company uses the authority-obedience system of management, there will be little opportunity for the man who has taken sensitivity training to apply what he has learned about collaboration and shared responsibility unless the president attends too. Possibly for this reason Douglas McGregor writes that "we must begin at the top," and that only when the superior becomes a consultant rather than an overseer does the organization become "devoted to expediting its business rather than to power struggles."

Professor Chris Argyris of Yale University adds a significant comment when he says: "Far too many current definitions . . . of what is best for an organization are shortsighted and obsolete. . . . Whether they survive in the long run will depend . . . on how well they can adapt themselves to meet the needs of . . . people."

Fortunately, most progressive company executives today no longer think in terms of "human engineering." The phrase itself has become obsolete with increasing awareness that the function of a human being in industry—at any level—cannot be likened to that of a cog in a wheel or a part in a machine. Increasingly, the managers of America's major corporations are learning that "management by crisis" is not inevitable. They recognize that sensitivity can be developed and skills can be learned that will help them deal more effectively with interdepartmental conflict and interpersonal rivalry. Today many companies report far-reaching improvement in motivating their people toward company goals—toward strengthening the organization and contributing to its well-being as a direct result of the greater competence brought to their jobs by men who have attended the management development training labs.

Many studies have investigated the processes and results of lab training. Some have been concerned with the learning method, others with the lasting effect of the T-group experience, and still others with a total evaluation of the laboratory experience. Considerable research is under way, in short, and much is still needed. But the evidence to date from both experience and investigation confirms our assumptions about the practical necessity of lab training for the business manager who must get things done through people.

Informal studies of the effectiveness of sensitivity training indicate that about 70 per cent of the participants find it has greatly improved their managerial competence. Many of these refer to the lab experience as "the most important three weeks of my adult life." About 20 per cent are not certain of the outcome but feel they would not want to have missed the experience. The remaining 10 per cent report no significant improvement.

Here are some of the benefits people say they take away with them:

1. A sense of confidence they've never in their lives had before.
2. A sense of really knowing more about themselves and others.
3. A new feeling of how to deal with the boss—or an associate who is very much like the boss. Some even report improvements in family situations.
4. A sense of being a more complete person.

The comments of several actual members follow. The names of the writers and their companies are authentic. The sentiments are typical of those expressed by a vast number of men who have taken sensitivity training over the past ten years.

From Earl Harris, president of the Rodney Hunt Machine Company:

> Taking the course was one of the most profoundly valuable experiences of my adult life. . . . It was tremendously helpful to my relationships with others in my work and in my family; to my other social relationships; and, not the least important, to my relationship with myself. It helped me to know myself.

> The course made me aware that my image in the minds and feelings of others was quite different from what I thought it to be or meant it to be. . . . Now I am much more conscious of my impact on another person and aware of his impact on me. I am aware of the importance of this in developing our attitudes toward each other.

> I believe I have become more tolerant and more understanding. [The course] has contributed to far more rewarding experiences with others, from close business associates to strangers.

From Robert E. Reese, research director of the *Detroit News:*

> I am indeed appreciative of what I believe I gained. . . . Particularly I feel indebted to the staff members—dedicated and totally selfless people. . . . A really valuable undertaking for any person with management responsibilities at any level of management. I would recommend it, based on my own experience, without any reservation whatsoever.

From Joseph H. Ellender, petroleum executive:

> If I had to sum up what one gets from sensitivity training, I would emphasize "truth" in a character sense: truth about one's own character and truth about one's relationship with others.

From William B. Covert, vice president of Amsted Industries:

> The experiences gained meant a new way of doing a more effective job in the art of management. Of greatest value were the increased understanding of human behavior, a better knowledge of the involved process of communication, and a much better insight into myself.

It is a major aim of lab training to link knowledge with application, especially to everyday operating problems. As we have seen, some of the management procedures, problems, and techniques which participants study include nondirective interviewing; role playing; committee leadership; decision making; team effectiveness; managerial styles; conflict resolution; performance reviews; and organization improvement.

Reports from subordinates and associates are another source of feedback, possibly a more objective one than personal testimony. Here is first-hand evidence of some of the changes most frequently observed in the job situation.

The lab participant:

- Has more confidence in what he's doing . . . is calmer, more relaxed, easier to work with, resolves conflicts with less irritation, is more interested in his relationships with others.
- Really listens when people talk to him now . . . does less needling, encourages group problem solving, is more patient, issues fewer orders, gets along better with others, doesn't fly off the handle.
- Seems to be less stubborn, doesn't supervise as closely, is more open to suggestions, more amenable to criticism, doesn't get angry as often, is more sensitive to the feelings of others.
- Works much more with groups now than before . . .

encourages participation in decisions, doesn't dominate meetings, is better able to delegate responsibility, gives more responsibility to subordinates.

Robert R. Blake and Jane S. Mouton of the University of Texas have suggested that sensitivity training "may well carry more promise for the amelioration of social problems than any other current treatment method, including education, counseling, social work, or psychotherapy." Other authorities have called lab training the most significant educational innovation of the century, the most important social invention in many decades, and a revolution in the behavioral sciences that is producing a science of management that can be taught and learned.

This would seem to indicate the enormous potential for the social good which more and more people believe sensitivity training offers. Pertinent, too, is this comment taken from a letter written by T-group graduate E. H. Cooley after returning home early in 1964 from a sensitivity-training experience. Mr. Cooley is president of Precision Cast Parts Corporation, of Portland, Oregon.

It [sensitivity training] has assisted me in improving the effectiveness with which our whole management team works together. I believe the benefits of this are visible in our profit and loss statements.

But Ed Cooley is not only the head of a company. Like most T-group participants, he is the head of a family as well. So he adds:

There are definite personal benefits for the individual [lab trainee] too. I would very much doubt that there is a man who has been through sensitivity training and, as a result, has not improved his relationship with his own wife and probably the rest of his family as well.

The record clearly justifies further developing and diversifying the scope of laboratory training. So far, it appears to offer the most hopeful method devised to help management in its dealing with people—its most important asset. The application of the scientific principles of human behavior to the management of men can have an impact that deserves the term "revolutionary." It can play a vital part in helping organizations prosper and survive by putting into full focus the human side of the picture—the feelings, emotions, and personal relationships that must be dealt with to achieve organizational success.

BIBLIOGRAPHY

BOOKS

Argyris, Chris, *Integrating the Individual and the Organization*, John Wiley & Sons, New York, 1964.

———, *Interpersonal Competence and Organizational Effectiveness*, The Dorsey Press, Homewood, Illinois, 1962.

———, *Personality and Organization: The Conflict Between System and the Individual*, Harper & Brothers, New York, 1957.

Asch, S. E., " Effects of Group Pressure" in *Groups, Leadership and Men: Research in Human Relations*, Carnegie Press, Pittsburgh, 1951.

Bennis, Warren G., Kenneth D. Benne, and Robert Chin, eds., *The Planning of Change: Readings in the Applied Behavioral Sciences*, Holt, Rinehart and Winston, New York, 1961.

Blake, Robert R., and Mouton, Jane S., *Group Dynamics: Key to Decision Making*, Gulf Publishing Company, Houston, Texas, 1961.

———, *The Managerial Grid*, Gulf Publishing Company, Houston, Texas, 1964.

———, *Training for Decision-Making Groups*, University of Texas, Austin, Texas, 1958.

Bradford, Leland P., ed., *Group Development*, National Training Laboratories, National Education Association, Washington, D.C., 1961.

Bradford, Leland P., Jack R. Gibb, and Kenneth D. Benne, *T-Group & Laboratory Method*, John Wiley & Sons, New York, 1964.

Cartwright, Dorwin, and Zander, Alvin, *Group Dynamics: Research and Theory*, Row, Peterson & Company, Evanston, Illinois, 1953.

Haire, Mason, ed., *Modern Organization Theory: A Symposium of the Foundation for Research on Human Behavior*, John Wiley & Sons, New York, 1959.

Lewin, Kurt, "Frontiers in Group Dynamics" in *Field Theory in Social Science*, Harper & Brothers, New York, 1951.

————, *Resolving Social Conflicts: Selected Papers on Group Dynamics,* Harper & Brothers, New York, 1948.

Likert, Rensis, *New Patterns of Management,* McGraw-Hill, New York, 1961.

Lippitt, Ronald, *Training in Community Relations,* Harper & Brothers, New York, 1949.

Maier, Norman R. F., *Principles of Human Relations*: *Applications to Management,* John Wiley & Sons, New York, 1952.

Marrow, A. J., *Making Management Human,* McGraw-Hill, New York, 1957.

McGregor, Douglas, *The Human Side of Enterprise,* McGraw-Hill, New York, 1960.

National Training Laboratories, *An Annotated Bibliography of Research, 1947-1960,* National Education Association, Washington, D.C., 1960.

National Training Laboratory in Group Development, *Explorations in Human Relations Training: An Assessment of Experience. 1947-1953,* National Education Association, Washington, D.C., 1953.

Tannenbaum, R., I. R. Weschler, and F. Massarik, *Leadership and Organization: A Behavioral Science Approach,* McGraw-Hill, New York, 1961.

Thelen, Herbert A., *The Dynamics of Groups at Work,* The University of Chicago Press, Chicago, 1954.

————, *Education and the Human Quest,* Harper & Brothers, New York, 1960.

Weschler, I. R., and Schein, E. H., *Issues in Human Relations,* National Training Laboratories, National Education Association, Washington, D.C., 1962.

ARTICLES AND PAMPHLETS

Argyris, Chris, "T-Groups for Organizational Effectiveness," *Harvard Business Review,* March-April 1964.

Benne, Kenneth D., and Whitman, R. M., "A Seminar on T-Group Aspects," National Training Laboratory, Bethel, Maine, 1953.

Bennis, Warren G., and Miles, M. B., "Report of National Laboratories' Committee on Trainer Development," National Training Laboratories mimeographed report, National Education Association, Washington, D.C., 1960.

Bennis, Warren G., Richard L. Burke, H. Cutter, H. Harrington, and J. Hoffman, "A Note on Some Problems of Measurement and Prediction in a Training Group," *Group Psychotherapy*, 1957.

Bennis, Warren G., and Peabody, D., "The Conceptualization of Two Personality Orientations and Sociometric Choice," *Journal of Social Psychology*, 1962.

Bennis, Warren G., and Slater, Philip E., "Democracy is Inevitable," *Harvard Business Review*, March-April 1964.

Blake, Robert R., Jane S. Mouton, and M. G. Blansfield, "How Executive Team Training Can Help You and Your Organization," *Journal of the American Society of Training Directors*, January 1962.

Blake, Robert R., Jane S. Mouton, and B. Fruchter, "A Factor Analysis of Training Group Behavior," *Journal of Social Psychology*, in press.

Burke, Richard L., and Bennis, Warren G., "Changes in Perception of Self and Others During Human Relations Training," *Human Relations*, May 1961.

Foundation for Research on Human Behavior, "An Action Research Program for Organization Improvement," Ann Arbor, March 1960.

French, J. R. P., Jr., "Role-playing as a Method of Training Foremen," *Sociometry*, 1945.

French, J. R. P., Jr., I. C. Ross, S. Kirby, J. R. Nelson, and P. Smythe, "Employee Participation in a Program of Industrial Change," *Personnel*, November-December 1958.

Likert, Rensis, "Measuring Organizational Performance," *Harvard Business Review*, March-April 1958.

Likert, Rensis, Chris Argyris, J. March, and H. Shepard, "Management Implications of Recent Social Science Research— A Symposium," *Personnel Administration*, May-June 1958.

Tannenbaum, R., "Dealing with Ourselves Before Dealing with Others, *Office Executive*, August 1957.

Weschler, I. R., and Reisel, J., "Inside a Sensitivity Training Group," Industrial Relations Monograph Number 4, Institute of Industrial Relations, University of California, Los Angeles, 1959.